Barriers to
Corporate Growth

Barriers to Corporate Growth

Barry D. Baysinger
Roger E. Meiners
Carl P. Zeithaml

Texas A&M University

LexingtonBooks
D.C. Heath and Company
Lexington, Massachusetts
Toronto

71119

To Becky, Chris, and Val

Library of Congress Cataloging in Publication Data

Baysinger, Barry D
    Barriers to corporate growth.

    Bibliography: p.
    Includes index.
    1. Corporations—Growth. I. Meiners, Roger E. II. Zeithaml, Carl P.
III. Title
HD2746.B39   658.4′06   80-8603
ISBN 0-669-04323-0   AACR2

Copyright © 1981 by D.C. Heath and Company

All rights reserved. No part of this publication may be reproduced or transmitted in any form or by any means, electronic or mechanical, including photocopy, recording, or any information storage or retrieval system, without permission in writing from the publisher.

Published simultaneously in Canada

Printed in the United States of America

International Standard Book Number: 0-669-04323-0

Library of Congress Catalog Card Number: 80-8603

Contents

List of Figures and Tables

Preface and
Acknowledgments

Why do some organizations grow to be very large while others remain stagnant? What internal and external factors promote organizational growth? What are the internal and external constraints on the growth of organizations? Although the issues contained in these questions have profound implications for many aspects of business theory and practice, the answers to them are limited and dispersed. Theory and research in the fields of management, economics, law, and finance have produced a modest literature concerning the growth and development of the organization. There is a particular deficiency in the understanding of the growth cycle of small firms and the various factors that contribute to the frustration of normal progress.

Since growth is viewed as a legitimate and often desirable objective for organizations to pursue, the absence of extensive research on this topic is somewhat surprising. Both academicians and practitioners appreciate the importance of organizational growth. For example, Pfeffer (1978) argues that growth increases the likelihood of an organization's survival and cites three advantages of growth. First, large organizations are not permitted to fail, as small businesses are. Because of their size and impact on society, firms such as Lockheed and Chrysler remain in operation even when extraordinary measures, such as political intervention, are required. Second, internal conflict is less likely under conditions of constant organizational expansion. Growth is usually accompanied by an increasing pool of resources, and individual members receive more resources in absolute terms. Conflict over the relative size of resource shares becomes a more salient issue as growth stops and contraction begins. Finally, growth provides the organization with more power relative to its environment. Greater control over the environment gives the firm the opportunity to engage in a more favorable resource exchange, thus reducing conflict and allowing for further growth. These advantages highlight the importance of understanding the growth process of organizations from both a business-policy and a public-policy perspective.

Given the significance of the growth issue, it appears that the shortage of growth-related research is a consequence of two problems. First, the limited theory and research that examines the organizational growth process is scattered throughout several disciplines. There has been no recent, comprehensive attempt to integrate and summarize the concepts and results contained in the literature that focuses on growth and growth-related topics. In particular, little effort has been directed toward identifying the barriers to growth and linking these constraints to the growth process. It would be useful to synthesize the growth literature from economics, organization theory, strategic management, law, finance, and small- and new-venture management. This synthesis might indicate some directions for investigation and, presumably, provide an identity for the organizational-growth literature.

The second problem involves the practical an methodological drawbacks to this research. There are inherent difficulties associated with studies of dynamic concepts, as well as problems of longitudinal data collection and analysis. These problems are not insurmountable, however, particularly with the trend toward a more sophisticated use of case studies, public business records, and comprehensive data bases (Hofer 1973; Miller and Friesen 1977; Schoeffler 1977). Innovative research techniques, together with a practitioner willingness to participate in growth studies, should alleviate this problem.

The purpose of this book, therefore, is to address the first of these problems, especially as it relates to the subject of the barriers to organizational growth. Chapter 1 provides an overview of the organizational growth process, drawing particularly on the organization-theory and strategic-management literatures. It discusses definitions and measures of growth, motives for growth, various models of the growth process, general barriers to growth, and some of the consequences attributed to growth. Chapter 2 increases the emphasis on barriers to organizational growth. A framework, or taxonomy, is developed and is used in subsequent chapters to classify the barriers or limits to growth drawn from the literature. Chapters 3 through 6 describe in detail the four classes of growth barriers outlined in chapter 2, synthesizing the relevant literature from various disciplines. Chapters 7 and 8 focus on two specific issues related to organizational growth. Chapter 7 studies the impact of state securities regulations on the firm growth process, and chapter 8 examines the implications of and comments on the experience curve phenomenon. In many of the chapters, suggestions are made for further research on the growth process. The suggestions are not intended to represent an exhaustive list of research topics. They are included to demonstrate the potential for work in this area and to encourage collaborative efforts by researchers with diverse backgrounds.

Finally, the reader is requested to make allowances for the interdisciplinary nature of the subject matter in this book. An effort has been made to minimize the use of unnecessary jargon and discipline-specific concepts. As a result, some terms may lack the precision normally required. For example, the terms *organization, business*, and *firm* are used interchangeably. Those who have attempted to integrate theory and research from diverse fields are aware of these difficulties.

Acknowledgments

Each of the authors developed an interest in the organizational growth process and barriers to growth through previous work in their different academic fields. Their original interdisciplinary collaboration on the topic, focusing on constraints on the life cycle of organizations, was supported by grants from the Small Business Administration and the Federal Trade Commission. This book represents a significant expansion of that effort.

The authors wish to thank the Small Business Administration and the Federal Trade Commission for their funding and assistance on the original project. However, this work in no way represents the views and policies of the SBA or the FTC.

1

An Overview of the Firm Growth Process

Organizational growth is a topic that has been addressed directly (Penrose 1959; Starbuck 1965, 1971; Tracy 1975; Filley, House, and Kerr 1976; Galbraith and Nathanson 1978) and in the context of other issues (Bain 1956; Hall 1972; Child 1977; Caves and Porter 1977). In most instances, growth has been cited as a common business objective or mentioned in discussions of organization size, organizational design, organizational performance, or barriers to the entry and exit of markets. Empirical research typically has not employed growth as a dynamic, continuous variable; rather, it has been referred to as the precursor to other static, discreet variables.

The purpose of this chapter is to examine the concept of growth and to review important models of the growth process. Since a tremendous portion of the management and economics literature relates in some way to the concept of organizational growth, it is difficult to include all references to the subject. The authors have attempted to summarize the major streams of the literature, however, and to include representative works from each area.

What Is Growth?

In his review of the literature on organizational size, Kimberly (1976) commented that conceptual definitions of size were lacking and that most of the definitions of size have been inferred from operational definitions. Since there is obviously a link between the organizational size and organizational growth literatures, it should be no surprise that a similar situation exists when one is considering definitions of organizational growth.

Ford and Slocum (1977) suggested that there are two types of definitions or measures of size: those that focus on the size of the organization and those that focus on the size of the organization's domain and/or its task environment. This dichotomy is generally applicable to the definitions of organizational growth found in the literature. Many of the definitions or measures of growth fall into two categories: First, growth is an increase in the size of the firm itself as measured by number of employees, net assets, sales volume, physical capacity, or the present value

1

of productive resources; and second, growth is an increase in the domain of the firm as measured by market share, size of the served market, or number of customers. In some cases, however, the characteristics of various stages in the growth process are described, and the author does not select a single definition or measure of growth. These studies appear to view growth as a multidimensional construct. Table 1-1 summarizes the operational definitions or measures of organizational growth that have been employed explicitly or implicitly in selected major works.

It is often difficult to determine the rationale for the definition employed in many of these growth studies. For example, Starbuck (1965, 1971) defined growth as a "change in an organizations's size when size is measured by the organization's membership or employment." No reason is offered for this definition. It is interesting to note that other readings in *Organizational Growth and Development* (1971) edited by Starbuck employed different measures and definitions of organizational growth. The operational definition or measure of growth used in a study may be a matter of access or convenience, or it may depend on the objective or context of the research. Studies that relate growth to the design of the organization tend to define growth in terms of internal measures of size such as number of employees. Conversely, studies that are interested in strategic influences on the organization—environment relationship often define growth as a change in market share. While the variety of definitions may make it more difficult to compare, contrast, and synthesize previous theoretical and empirical efforts, Hall (1972, p. 111) suggested that measures of *size* appear to be "interchangeable for research and operational purposes." There is also some empirical evidence that measures of size (and, therefore, growth) may be highly related (Child 1973; Pugh et al. 1969).

For the purposes of this book, growth is defined as an increase in the present value of an organization's resources due to conscious management decisions. This definition is developed fully in chapter 2. Briefly, it was selected for three reasons. First, it is consistent with the economic concepts employed in the analysis of barriers to organizational growth in chapters 2 through 6. Second, it is a multidimensional, conceptual definition of growth since it recognizes that growth entails more than individual measures of human and physical resources, production costs, or market demand. Third, although it is conceptual, it can be operationalized for measurement. Growth of this nature is reflected by an increase in the market value of outstanding equity shares. Despite the use of this definition, there continues to be an opportunity for further conceptual development and increased precision. Many of the considerations discussed by Kimberly in his paper on organizational size may be relevant in this area as well.

Table 1-1
Selected Works on Organizational Growth (and Size) Classified by Operational Definition or Measure of Growth

Number of Employees	Assets	Sales Volume	Capacity	Market Share	Multidimensional
Graicunas (1937)	Ijiri and Simon (1967)	Ijiri and Simon (1967)	Simon and Bonini (1958)	Schoeffler, Buzzel, and Heany (1974)	Penrose (1959)
Haire (1959)		Khandwalla (1977)			Scott (1971)
Starbuck (1965)				Buzzell, Gale, and Sultan (1975)	Filley, House, and Kerr (1976)
Hall, Haas, and Johnson (1967)					Child (1977)
Pugh et al. (1968)					Galbraith and Nathanson (1978)
Hickson et al. (1969)					
Blau (1970)					
Blau and Schoenherr (1971)					
Meyer (1972)					
Child (1973)					
Dewar and Hage (1978)					
Beyer and Trice (1979)					

Motives for Growth

There are many reasons for organizational growth. The literature agrees, however, that organizational growth is not a random phenomenon. It may result from strategic decisions implemented to achieve increased organizational size per se or as a by-product of strategies formulated to attain other goals. In a comprehensive review of the growth literature, Starbuck states that "the most widely accepted approach to growth has been that growth is either a means of attaining other goals or a side effect of such attainment, rather than an end in itself" (1971, p. 14). While growth may be pursued as a symbol of achievement or progress, it is related typically to the achievement of organizational or individual member goals.

Specifically, Starbuck (1971, pp. 15-32) enumerates ten managerial motives that have been related to growth:

1. Organizational self-realization (fulfilling the potential of the organization)
2. Adventure and risk (desire to gamble on new activities and avoid boredom)
3. Prestige, power, and job security (greater prestige and power is attached to the supervision of a large number of people)
4. Executive salaries (management expands itself in order to increase its salaries)
5. Profit
6. Cost
7. Revenue
8. Monopolistic power
9. Stability (large organizations tend to face more stable environments than small organizations)
10. Survival

Obviously, many of these motives are interrelated, and their relative importance depends on the situation. It is critical to note, however, that these motives are necessary but not sufficient to produce growth, since they must overcome internal and external pressures to maintain the status quo or to decrease organizational size. Various bargaining and problem-solving processes are used to resolve the conflict between environmental contingencies, the skills and resources of the firm, and the attitudes of organizational members.

Child (1977) adds another perspective to the list of motives for organizatonal growth. While he concurs with several of the reasons listed by Starbuck, Child contends that growth is also a consequence of success. He argues that assets grow when a business returns a net surplus that is neither distributed completely nor set aside for depreciation. In such a case, a revenue or profit maximizing objective may lead to growth, rather than growth resulting in profit as suggested by some authors. It is evident that additional research is required to examine the reasons for growth, the causal relationships between critical variables, the factors that counteract these motives and inhibit growth, and the relationship between opposing sets of motives and growth.

Models of Growth

Several models have been developed for the purpose of explaining and describing the organizational growth process. These frameworks include a wide range of variables and represent thought from several fields of management. Since growth models usually are constructed to examine particular issues, they vary in approach and level of comprehension. Galbraith and Nathanson point out that "the problem with all of these models is not that they are wrong, but that they are only partially correct" (1978, p. 103).

Starbuck identified four categories of growth models (1965, 1971). Cell-division models are analogous to the continuous, smooth development models of biological growth (Haire 1959). They focus on growth as a percentage change in size and emphasize the prediction of total size over time. Metamorphic models view growth as abrupt and discrete changes in the activities, strategies, and structure of an organization, emphasizing changes in kind rather than degree (for example, Weber 1947; Bennet and McNight 1956; Lester 1958; Hoffer 1958; Rostow 1960; Filley 1962; Lippit and Schmidt 1967; Pugh et al., 1969; James 1973; Child 1977; Mintzbert 1979). Organizations are adaptive systems which assume configurations compatible with their goals and situational conditions. Will-o'-the-wisp models focus on growth as a process in which organizational members pursue some opportunity, resource, or advantage (for example, Penrose 1959). Finally, decision-process models attempt to reproduce the major decision rules used by organizations for the purposes of prediction (for example Cyert, Feigenbaum, and March 1959). While these models are potentially the most fruitful approach to explaining organizational growth, they tend to be quite limited because of the complexity of the growth-decision process.

The majority of growth models discussed in the organization theory and strategic management literature use the metamorphosis approach. Mintzberg argues that these models are more realistic as organizational growth is charactrized by clear structural transitions, "fundamental changes in the ways their work is divided and coordinated" (1979, p. 248). Two models of particular interest are suggested by Filley and his associates (1962, 1974,

1975, 1976, 1978) and Galbraith and Nathanson (1978). Each model examines numerous dimensions of the growth process; studied together they probably represent the "state-of-the-art" in growth-related theory and research.

Filley has developed an organizational typology based upon three adaptive strategies for organizing and dealing with the environment. The types are identified as craft, promotion, and administration. Each type consists of a pattern of structural and leadership characteristics which are observed together. Table 1-2 summarizes the characteristics of the three organization types.

The craft firm is dominated usually by the owner-manager. This individual is not interested in significant organizational growth and, instead, emphasizes survival and a reasonable return on investment. The successful craft firm operates generally in an environment that is neither hostile nor uncertain. It generally profits by the relative advantages asociated with its size, according to the particular industry and region. Since the craft firm exhibits low levels of risk taking and innovation, however, it does not adapt well to changes in the market environment. The internal operations and relationships of the business are fixed and governed by tradition and convention. There are low staffing needs for indirect labor and adequate levels of morale.

The promotion firm is dominated again by the chief executive, but the characteristics of this individual, and, therefore, of the business are quite different. The executive is typically a dynamic, charismatic individual, with high personal needs for achievement. The promotion firm follows the classic S-shaped pattern of growth, which is often related to the product life cycle. Innovation is responsible for the rapid growth of the promotion firm. It slows eventually when competitors enter the market, the market becomes saturated, or the effectiveness of the promoter declines. The organization attempts to exploit an innovative, unique product during the early part of the growth curve. Morale during this period is high, while policies and work functions are developed and implemented only as required.

The administrative firm has a professional management group that emphasizes formal planning and a structured, hierarchical organization. These firms grow at a rate that is consistent with the industry unless they are more or less effective than competitors in attracting business. The administrative firm adapts to changes in its market environment through product improvement as opposed to product innovation.

Filley and Aldag (1978) undertook an empirical test of the hypothesized characteristics of each organization type. Their analyses supported the typology, thus, suggesting that the classification, description, and study of organizations using a single criterion such as size or technology may not fully reveal significant differences. This also implies that it may not be

Table 1-2
Characteristics in Three Organization Types

Characteristic	Craft	Organization Type	
		Promotion	Administrative
Objectives	Comfort-survival	Personal achievement	Market Adaptation
Policy	Traditional	Personal	Rational
Leadership	Craftsman	Entrepreneur	Professional
Structure	Power levels	Field of force	Rational hierarchy
Staff	Housekeeping	Technical-personal	Technical-coordinative
Functional-development	Single	Successive emphasis	Full development
Work-group bonds	Fixed roles	Interaction-expectation	Homogeneity
Innovation	Conventional methods	Innovation	Development
Uncertainty-risk	No perceived risk	Uncertainty	Risk
Basis for success	Benevolent environment	Innovation exploitation	Planned adaptation to environment
Pattern of growth	Non-growth	S-curve	Linear

A.C. Filley and R.J. Aldag, "Characteristics and Measurement of an Organizational Typology," *Academy of Management Journal* 21 (1978):579-580.

appropriate to define growth operationally using a traditional, single measure; rather, it may be necessary to adapt a multidimensional construct.

Several caveats concerning this organizational typology are necessary. First, the characteristics of each type are merely associated with and are not necessarily the causes or effects of each type. While there may be a cause and effect relationship between the characteristics, empirical research does not address this point. Second, there is no required order in which the types must appear. For example, although the promotion stage is a period of transition, the firm may become either a craft or administrative type once its relative advantages end. Third, the patterns of growth suggested above for each type are not absolutely necessary. Alternative patterns are possible under certain conditions. Finally, Filley et al. (1976) conclude that previous studies (Haire 1959; Filley 1962; Starbuck 1968) suggest that there are regularities in the growth of organizations. Assuming that the firm makes no departure from its regular organization and product base, they contend that the pattern of growth can be predicted fairly well with a cell-division model. The natural course of growth can be altered, however, through deliberate reorganization or changes in management processes.

Galbraith and Nathanson recently developed an alternate metamorphosis model of organizatonal growth (1978). The Galbraith-Nathanson model integrates and revises earlier models and empirical research focused on the relationships between the strategy, structure, and performance of the organization (Chandler 1962; Stopford 1968; Wrigley 1970; Channon 1971, 1973; Scott 1971; Pooley-Dias 1972; Thanheiser 1972; Stopford and Wells 1972; Franko 1974, 1976; Rumelt 1974). The model (figure 1-2) indicates the alternate paths followed by organizations as they develop from single product, single function firms to complex diversified and/or integrated organizations.

The model illustrates the authors' belief that firms follow a developmental sequence characterized by a metamorphosis between stages. While the model allows for alternate paths, not all paths are possible. For example, a simple functional organization cannot become a global multinational without passing through at least one transitional form. There is no requirement that a firm must continue to evolve. The growth process may stagnate if management is satisfied with present performance levels or if it is unable or unwilling to manage further diversity. As a result, Galbraith and Nathanson prefer to refer to these states as types of organization forms.

Like the Filley model of organizational growth, the Galbraith and Nathanson model describes each organizational stage or type in terms of certain characteristics. As organizations grow through simple, functional, holding, multidivisional, and global types, they evolve along a number of dimensions. At a corporate level, the product strategy develops from a single product to multiple products in multiple countries. This growth may

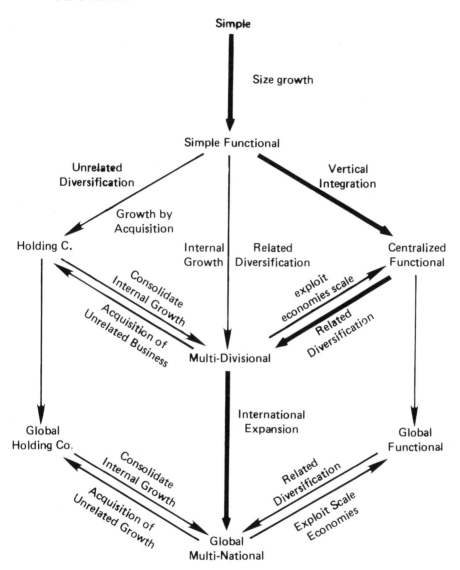

Reproduced by permission from *Strategy Implementation: The Role of Structure and Process*, by Jay R. Galbraith and Daniel A. Nathanson. Copyright © 1978, West Publishing Company.

Figure 1-1. Galbraith and Nathanson Revised Growth Model

take place by acquisition and/or internal growth. Organization structure undergoes several transitions ranging from more centralized, functionally organized designs to decentralized profit centers around worldwide product or area divisions. Research and development becomes increasingly institutionalized and located in centers of expertise. Performance measures shift from personal, subjective criteria to impersonal, objective, multiple goals tailored to the product and country. Other characteristics that change with growth include interunit and market relations, rewards, careers, leader style and control, and the types of strategic choices to be made by top management. The specification of these characteristics indicates that Galbraith and Nathanson subscribe to a multidimensional view of organizational growth.

The only other growth models of interest are found occasionally in the small and new venture management literature. Once again, these models fall primarily into the metamorphosis category of growth models. Examples of these typologies include: (1) start-up firms, early-growth firms, and later-growth firms (Cooper 1979); (2) survival firms, attractive growth potential firms, underachieving firms, and high success firms (Susbauer 1979); (3) direct supervision, supervised supervisor, indirect control, and divisional organization (Steinmetz 1969); and (4) the managerial stages in the development of a small business such as a one person operation, the separation of management and nonmanagement functions, and the separation of ownership and management functions, (Megginson 1961). Most of these models focus on the changing processes of management, the changing role of the entrepreneur, and the competitive and innovative strategies typically associated with the growth stages or types of firms. They tend to be quite descriptive (usually based on case studies) and to reflect the opinions of their authors. The characteristics associated with these models are very similar to those discussed by Filley. Despite the importance of empirical research examining the characteristics and patterns of small business development, there are few studies which make a contribution in this area.

Barriers to Growth

While research on the organizational growth process is limited, there is even less research devoted explicitly to the examination of barriers to organizational growth. Although chapters 2 through 7 are devoted explicitly to a discussion of this subject, several brief comments are appropriate at this point. A number of authors identify particular reasons why organizations fail to grow, but there is no comprehensive summary or categorization of these factors. Susbauer suggests one potentially useful way to approach the topic (1979). He contends that in order for firms to grow they must possess both a growth potential and a growth orientation. Growth potential depends on external factors (such as the rate of market expansion), while growth orientation generally refers to the aspirations and abilities of management relative to growth. Growth potential is a prerequisite to growth, but it is not sufficient for its realization.

Based on these concepts, two lists of barriers to growth can be created. One list contains those factors which retard growth potential; the second lists factors which inhibit a growth orientation. Prior to enumerating these factors, one caveat is required: the following lists could be condensed since many of these barriers to growth are interrelated. However it is the intention of this discussion to present the wide spectrum of barriers to growth as drawn from the literatures of interest. The discussion contained in the following chapters should further integrate and relate these barriers both to each other and to the process in general.

The following factors limit the growth potential of the organization:

1. The products and services offered by the firm and their attributes (price, quality, and so forth) fail to match the particular needs of the growth market.
2. There is a stable or declining demand for the product offering of the firm.
3. Overcapacity and/or supply exist in the marketplace (that is, a buyer's market).
4. Legal or regulatory restrictions of the growth of the firm impede growth.
5. General macro-economic conditions restrict growth opportunities (for example, shortage of investment funding).
6. Negative image of the firm results in societal sanctions inhibiting growth (for example, total product line boycotted due to poor image of single product offering).

The following factors inhibit the growth orientation of the firm:

1. General lack of management expertise and skill
2. Shortage of working capital to obtain resources for growth or to penetrate markets
3. Late entry into growth market
4. Conscious avoidance of growth
5. Overspecialization of management
6. Conscious failure or inability to recruit and/or train growth-oriented management
7. Lack of coordination between production and marketing (for example, too few products, diversifying too quickly)
8. Financial mismanagement

9. Inventory mismanagement
10. Lack of market research, advertising, and proper selling techniques
11. Personal problems of management (for example, poor health, family problems)
12. Inability of management to control increased complexity and diversity of operations
13. Fraudulent behavior
14. Lack of information concerning where to obtain expansion financing or lack of willingness to do so

It is clear that these lists are neither exhaustive nor mutually exclusive; they simply are intended to be preliminary categorizations of common barriers to growth. It is obvious that a major research emphasis should be given to these factors and their actual relevance to the growth process. Once again, empirical research on this topic is virtually nonexistent.

Consequences of Growth

Management scholars and practitioners typically view organizational growth as a positive phenomenon. As discussed earlier, growth can improve the likelihood of survival, reduce internal conflict, and enhance organizational power and control. Growth, particularly in terms of market share, also has been linked to profitability. Researchers associated with the Strategic Planning Institute have found strong empirical support for the proposition that market share is positively related to the rate-of-return on investment earned by a business (Buzzell, Gale, and Sultan 1975). These and similar findings have suggested that firms should implement strategies designed to increase market share.

Despite this conventional belief, many authors caution that firms considering a growth objective should be aware of two points: First growth is not necessarily related to improved organizational performance, and, second, even when growth ultimately improves performance, there are usually substantial costs, financial and otherwise, associated with the growth process. Several studies conclude that growth-related strategies can result in disaster for the firm involved (Chevalier 1972; Fruhan 1972; Hammeresh, Anderson, and Harris 1978). An approach which emphasizes maximizing return on invested capital in small, defensible market segments or "niches" in which the firm possesses some distinctive competence or competitive advantage is preferable in many situations. Low market-share companies in many industries consistently outperform the large firms, indicating that there are viable and profitable alternatives to growth.

Firms should also be aware of the costs associated with the growth process. Research completed at the Strategic Planning Institute indicates that growth requires cash because of increased investment (Schoeffler 1977). Because capital-intensive businesses usually cannot generate this cash internally, obvious difficulties are added to their growth plans. Hall also points out that growth often brings new members into the organization and upsets existing patterns of interaction and communication (1972). As coordination becomes more difficult, increases in formalization and routinization typically occur. These alternatives in the social and power structure and in the design of work can be quite threatening to veteran members of the firm. It is critical that such issues are confronted, examined, and accounted for prior to the initiation of the growth process.

Finally, growth has been related to structural changes in the organization. In his review of the literature on organizational size, Mintzberg (1979, p. 234) concluded that increased size (measured typically by number of employees) may result in greater specialization, greater differentiation between organizational units, more levels in the hierarchy, less need for intraunit coordination, more need for interunit coordination, large unit size, more formalization of behavior, more use of planning and control system, and, ultimately, more bureaucracy. These factors obviously are interrelated, and they will occur in varying degrees depending on other situational influences such as the technical system employed and the growth rate itself. Organizations also experience structural transitions with growth as demonstrated by the Galbraith-Nathanson model. Once again, these structural changes appear to follow the metamorphosis pattern.

This brief overview of the concepts and models of organizational growth is intended to familiarize the reader with general issues in the literature. With this background, the remainder of the book focuses on the issue of specific interest, barriers to organizational growth.

2 A Taxonomy of Barriers to Firm Growth

The discussion of organizational growth in the previous chapter identifies a number of the important constraints or barriers to growth. A review of the existing literature indicates that it may be very difficult, if not impossible, to overcome some of these barriers. In many cases continued smallness is consistent with normal progress, or, where it is not, represents a fact of life which cannot be remedied without incurring high costs. Therefore, the primary objective of the next five chapters is to identify remediable limits to the normal growth of small business enterprises in the United States, as reflected in the scholarly literature concerning the growth and development of the business enterprise in general.

The purpose of this chapter is to develop a framework or taxonomy that may be used to classify all barriers to the growth of small businesses that are discussed in existing works. Once the framework has been described, each barrier to normal growth may be discussed as an analytically distinct category with references to the literature relevant to that category. This approach emphasizes the distinction between remediable and nonremediable limits to the growth of small firms.

Definitions: The Firm, Growth, and Its Limits

A discussion of the business firm must begin with a specification of the concept of the firm to be employed. This is necessary because the concept of the business firm differs according to the problem. Moreover, while one definition of the firm may be highly useful for clear understanding in one context, that same definition may be inimical to clear understanding in other contexts. A prime example of this is the distinction between the concept of the firm that is appropriate for much economic theory and that appropriate to discussion of business growth and development.

Determining the prices of resources and their allocation among various uses is one of the central problems of theoretical economics. To this end, "the appropriate model of the *firm* is a model representing the forces determining the prices and quantities produced of particular products in the individual firm" (Penrose 1959, p. 11). Such a model reduces to a cost and revenue function for a single product. The profit maximizing equilibrium of the firm determines the level of output and prices for the particular output of the firm. The limits to growth of the firm under this definition

15

are found simply in the shape of the cost and revenue functions. Although the functions are different for each firm, in all cases the firm stops growing when the upward sloping marginal cost function intersects the downward sloping marginal revenue function (which is derived directly from the demand curve a firm faces for its product). While useful for particular problems of economic analysis, this concept of the firm does not promote understanding in a world where cost and revenue functions may be acted upon and changed by conscious entrepreneurial design. In these firms, especially in the size range of interest here, cost and revenue functions cannot generally be treated as true barriers to new growth.

From the view of theoretical economic analysis, what most people would identify as a business firm would be a series of firms. That is, what is commonly called a firm has many more attributes than simply a cost and revenue function. This, however, does not mean that the nature of the firm cannot be reduced to a manageable abstraction for the purpose of discussing limits to growth. In fact a highly useful abstract definition holds simply that the firm is the absence of market-mediated exchange in commercial intercourse (Coase 1937). This view recognizes that all production and exchange could conceivably be organized through market transactions, but this mode of organization will be abandoned whenever the costs of allocating resources by administrative decisions are lower than the costs associated with using markets. In this sense, firms grow by substituting administrative commands for market prices. But a clear understanding of what firms are and how they grow requires more than a statement of what they are not.

To this end, Penrose has defined the firm as "a collection of productive resources the disposal of which is determined by administrative decision" (1959, p. 24). This definition is consistent with that of Coase but adds the idea of the firm as a collection of human and physical resources. From this, firm growth and size may be defined with respect to the resources administered by conscious management decisions.

The size of a firm simply refers to the present value of the resources directed by an autonomous administrator. This value can be changed by adding resources or more effectively managing the resources on hand. Firms grow whenever the present value of the resources increases due to conscious administration. This is a useful definition in that it gives explicit recognition to a variety of factors which influence the development of firms aside from simple considerations of market demand, production cost, or the presence of human and physical resources. So defined, the limits to the growth of small firms may be shown to be elsewhere than in the slope properties of the cost and revenue functions. While these place limits on the growth of very large firms, they need not be considered as barriers to the normal growth of firms in the early stages of their life cycle.

As indicated previously, the firm as described in economic theory grows by increasing output until the long-run marginal costs of production rise to equality with marginal revenue. For any product (or product group) that can be produced using a given physical plant, the limit to growth is given by the law of diminishing marginal returns (for perfectly competive firms) and the firms law of demand (for firms with market power and, hence, downward sloping demand curves). Such limits are necessary if a determinant equilibrium price and output is to be derived, and the economic definition is perfectly appropriate for the intended theoretic purposes. However, invoking the law of diminishing marginal returns requires the existence of some fixed factor of production. That factor is assumed to be management. The limit to growth of the firm becomes a matter of the inability of management to coordinate production activities over a certain size and complexity. This ignores the possibility that managerial innovation overcomes the limit to firm size. Moreover, as Penrose observed, the "fact that demand curves for given *products* can be assumed to be tilted downward does not mean that the expected net revenue from additional units of *investment* need ever become negative . . . To say that the expansion of a firm which can produce unspecified new products is limited by 'demand', is to say that there are not products that the firm could produce profitably" (1959, p. 13). Thus, one may conclude that the limits to firm growth must be found in something other than the fixity of managerial talent and the first law of demand. That is, if such limits exist they apply as absolute barriers to the growth of firms which have grown to a size beyond the interests of this research.

As collections of administered productive resources, firms may grow by taking advantage of productive opportunities that comprise "all of the productive possibilities that (their) 'entrepreneurs' see and can take advantage of" (Penrose 1959, p. 31). Firms may advertise, add new product lines, and engage in organizational innovations in an effort to grow, that is, to increase the present value of the collection of productive resources administered. Thus, it follows that the limits to growth may be defined in terms of a failure either to see or take advantage of productive opportunities. Of firms in an early stage of their life cycle, it may be asserted that the limit to growth is found elsewhere than in an exhaustion of productive opportunities. Unlike the firm of economic theory, there is nothing, in principle, fixed about the factor of production known as management. There are always ways for administrative innovation to push outward the point of managerial diseconomies of scale. Likewise, there are always ways, in principle, for firms in the early stage of development to gain market-share or create new markets for the products they could produce. Whether or not the management of small firms are able to see, or to take advantage of, their productive possibilities is another question. It is the key question to be addressed here.

To summarize, the nature of the firm applicable to the question of determining the limits to growth is quite different from the firm of economic price theory. For this study, *firm* is defined as a collection of productive resources allocated to their highest valued uses by administrative decisions rather than by market prices. Firms so defined are not limited to single production and revenue functions and, hence, their growth potential is not determined by the law of diminishing marginal returns, organizational scale diseconomies, or a falling marginal return on sales. These absolute limits to the growth of firms are relevant to business units much larger than those of concern here. Firms in the early stages of their life cycles grow by increasing the present value of the resources administered by an entrepreneur or management group. The productive opportunities of such firms are, in principle, unlimited. They include the ability to add new products and markets when existing products begin to face production diseconomies, market saturation, and the inability to construct organizational innovations to eliminate managerial diseconomies. Limits to firm growth are to be found in the failure or inability of those administering the productive resources of the firm to see or take advantage of these unlimited productive opportunities. A taxonomy of these limits to growth is presented next.

A Taxonomy of Barriers to the Growth of Small Firms

Interests in the limits to the growth of firms is, in an economic rather than political sense, synonymous with concern over the allocative inefficiency of monopoly. To be meaningful, limits to growth must refer to failed expectation; that is, for a discussion of limits to growth to be interesting it must involve a potential increase in the value of administered resources that failed to occur. Economists define monopoly in similar terms:

> To an economist, expansion of capacity either by *de nova* entrants or by established companies is entry in the meaningful sense of moving resources (capital and manpower) into the use in question. Monopoly in an economically functional sense means a situation where an industry fails to add resources when justified and called for by the demand and cost situation. If customers are willing to pay more for the additional product than the cost of using resources to produce more, and if these resources are not moved into the industry in question, then monopoly prevails and inefficiency is a consequence (Brozen 1975, p. 11).

For all intents and purposes, limits to the growth of firms and barriers to entry are one and the same. They refer to those circumstances where, on the basis of objective facts, one could reasonably expect something to occur but is, for some reason, disappointed. When an increase in the present value of firm resource is the phenomenon expected, the factors contributing to failed expectations may be considered a genuine barrier to entry or limit to growth.

It is important to note that for the purpose of disussing the limits to growth vis-à-vis the small firm, the existence of entry barriers is not necessarily indicative of an undesirable or disequilibrium situation. The existence of small firms which, on the basis of favorable environmental factors, one would have expected to grow into larger firms, may be due only to the fact that the entrepreneurs directing the firms' fortunes also own the enterprise and prefer their present size. However, in order to make the following discussion relevant for policy purposes, we will asume that the small firms of interest are owned by individuals who prefer growth where opportunities for growth exist. In a similar vein, it is improper to infer from the persistence of industrial smallness that entry barriers or limits to firm growth exist, and must necessarily be a problem. The normal life cycle of a variety of enterprises may not include growth to even moderate size because of the particular advantages of smallness. There are certain comparative advantages of small scale enterprise which have nothing to do with the absolute limits to firm growth. Moreover, even without such comparative advantages, when the growth of large firms in an industry is less than the growth of the economy or industry as a whole, there will be residual opportunities for small firms to exploit without increasing their size.

The comparative advantage of smallness falls into several categories. For example, the *Wall Street Journal* has noted that the greater decision-making flexibility of small enterprises allows them to take better advantage of unusual economic circumstances than larger firms. Small firms can react quickly to profitable opportunities, such as buying the inventories of firms in distress at bargain prices. Smaller firms also exploit the supervisory advantage of having less distance between the top and the bottom of the organization chart (3/13/80). Because managers can frequently deal directly with employees and are not tied to strict union contracts, they are not frustrated in efforts to increase productivity.

Other advantages cited include the ability to adjust prices rapidly in an inflationary economy, the better rapport owner-managers and owners of small firms can have with their employees, and the ability to shift product lines in the face of new market opportunities. Moreover, "industries involving style goods are dominated by smaller, more flexible companies. Industries requiring close coordination of skills are seldom large scale . . ." (Archer 1976, p. 50). Thus, a Penrose observed, in some respects small firms enjoy a persistent comparative advantage over larger firms: "Some kinds of activity are unsuited to large firms, for example, those requiring quick adaptation to changing conditions, close personal attention to detail, the whims of customers, etc." (1959, p. 220). Smallness is sometimes its own reward and not the result of entry barriers and other limits to growth. Therefore, barriers to new growth may not be deduced from the persistence of small scale enterprise alone.

Moreover, even in those cases where large firms enjoy a competitive advantage over their smaller rivals in the same industry, smallness may persist in the absence of any limits to growth. In a growing economy it may be the case that new opportunities for the growth of large firms occur faster than they can handle by expansion. If so, small firms may continue to fill the "interstices" left in the economy by the failure of large firms to grow as fast as the economic opportunities offered them. Therefore, the persistence over time of small firms in an industry may not necessarily be the result of limits to growth; rather, it may be the result of "excessive" increases in opportunities to prosper.

With this in mind we may limit discussion to the genuine limits to firm growth that have received attention in the literature. These, it will be recalled, involved failures to grow which resulted from the administrator-entrepreneur's failure to see, or inability to exploit, productive opportunities that were available. In terms of an organizational framework, we may consider all factors contributing to the observed persistence of smallness among business organizations. Figure 2-1 summarizes the classification scheme of these growth limits.

Within the broad category of growth limits there are two subcategories: one that refers to those factors which result in the *free choice of decision makers and owners to remain small* (for example, satisfaction with the status quo, the comparative advantages of smallness, or the position of filling the interstices in the economy), and another subcategory that refers to *genuine limits to growth or entry barriers* applicable to small firms. The latter category, which is or primary concern here, may be divided into two additional subcategories. First, some of the "problems" encountered by small firms which face exploitable productive opportunities are simply the natural consequences of being small, new, or inexperienced in business activity.

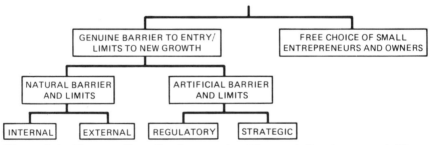

Figure 2-1. Factors Contributing to the Observed Persistence of Firm Smallness

These problems will be referred to as the *natural barriers* to expected growth. They are genuine and effectively frustrate the progress of firms desiring to increase the present value of the productive resources embodied in the enterprise, but they are not the result of human contrivance. Second, those factors which also genuinely limit the growth of small firms but which are the result of human contrivance will be termed *artificial barriers* to entry or limits to growth. These factors may be the inadvert consequences of the behavior of others, or they may represent the conscious efforts of others to retard growth by erecting barriers to entry. Both will be treated as artificial barriers to growth. Of the genuine limits to growth, we will distinguish among those attributable to the actions of others which have an adverse impact on small firms, either intentionally or inadvertently.

These two broad categories may be further subdivided. Under the natural barriers to new growth, two groups may be identified: those involving the *internal environment* of the firm and those involving *external environmental factors* which inhibit progress to greater size. Recall that firms will fail to develop, in general, whenever their decision makers "fail to see or take advantage of" productive opportunities. Internal natural limits to growth involve the failure to see, or to take advantage of these opportunities because of the quality of management. External natural limits refer to failures to take advantage of productive opportunities which do not involve managerial limitations. Basically, these external natural limits will involve some uncontrived restriction of the resources, especially financial capital, which are necessary for growth.

By their nature, all artificial barriers to entry and growth are external to the small enterprise. But within this category may be identified those barriers representing the by-products of public policy. It is assumed that public policies were designed to promote some social goal, but, inadvertently they have had an adverse impact on the normal progress of small enterprises. These inadvertent by-products of policy will be referred to as *regulatory barriers* to the progress of small firms. These limits may be sharply contrasted with the contrived anticompetitive behavior of other firms that is intended to limit energy. These contrived limits include some of the traditional barriers to entry common to industrial organization theory and are *strategic barriers* to entry and growth.

Four distinct classes of genuine limits to the growth of small enterprise have now been identified: natural-internal, natural-external, artificial-regulatory, and artificial-strategic. A final dichotomization is possible and involves separating factors limiting the growth of new firms which are remediable, either through public policy or concerted private action, from those which are not remediable, either because they represent a fact of life which cannot be overcome by conscious effort, or because their elimination imposes unacceptable costs on other sectors of the economy.

Any classification scheme will involve judgement, and not all readers will be in complete agreement with the way various factors are categorized. However, the taxonomy presented here has been constructed to emphasize the fact that the failure of small firms to develop into larger firms is not necessarily a problem, at least from an economic standpoint. From that view, the limits to growth that exist for small enterprise may or may not be a legitimate cause for public concern. The framework presented in this chapter forces the barriers to growth into categories that are most relevant for further research and public attention.

3 Natural-Internal Barriers to Firm Growth

Although the taxonomy developed in the last chapter lists natural-internal limits to growth as one of the four major divisions of the barriers to firm growth, it is the least important from the perspective of this study. It may be postulated that the primary reason many businesses fail to grow or prosper is because of managerial "failures" to exploit opportunities that may exist. However, such weaknesses on the part of entrepreneurs are generally not matters of public policy concern.

The primary natural-internal barriers to firm growth stem from managerial or entrepreneurial inadequacies. Organizations will suffer or fail to perform as well as they could simply because of ordinary human limitations of education, experience, foresight, ability, and personal preferences. Of these factors, education may be the only matter that can really be addressed through the use of public policy.

A large part of the study of business, particularly in the field of management, is directed toward an understanding of the structure and processes of organizations. Based on this knowledge, the role of business educators is to train prospective and current business practitioners. If the education has value, it would be expected that persons trained in the operation of private organizations would be able to outperform their counterparts who do not have such training. Therefore, one may argue that if more educational opportunities for managers and entrepreneurs were provided, personal inability due to lack of education would be diminished. However, educational opportunities are provided by the private sector whenever there is a demand for certain skills or information, and there are considerable additional opportunities already provided that are subsidized by the public. If individuals cannot or do not take advantages of opportunities to make their business enterprises more successful, there is nothing that outside observers can do about such missed chances. Furthermore, since business acumen may be developed either by formal training or by experience, it is difficult to partial out the effects of each and evaluate the relative contributions to performance. Since the purpose of this study is primarily to identify barriers to firm growth that are beyond the control of the individual and can be remedied, there may be little to be done in the area of business education from a public policy perspective.

Experience is something that can be gained only by practice within organizations over time. The process may be hastened by experienced persons' passing on the benefit of their knowledge via education or by informal contact within organizations. The application of experience to decisions that help firms prosper is, in part, specific to each organization and not a matter that can be addressed in general terms. In many cases, given the evolutionary nature of firms, there is no way to hasten or alter the experience process and stimulate its application to future opportunities.

Although it is often difficult to distinguish from luck, foresight or entrepreneurial talent may also be critical. Of those organizations that have prospered beyond the norm, it may be difficult to discern how much prosperity was due to clever decision making by managers, how much resulted from environmental factors beyond the control of the managers, and how much was due to plain luck. While education about business may study and relate various business success stories, there is still going to be an element of luck that influences the fate of some firms. The ability to predict where opportunities will arise often requires an entrepreneurial genius that some persons are simply fortunate enough to possess. The fact that most persons do not have such ability may be viewed as a natural-internal constraint to growth, but it is obviously something that cannot be addressed critically. In some instances, a person may have foresight, but be unable to translate that knowledge into action because of managerial inability or other circumstances that prevent the perceived opportunity from being exploited. As will be discussed later, this may be due to factors beyond the control of the individual, such as imperfections in the capital market. In other cases, it may result from differences in perception of the opportunity that the entrepreneur asserts to exist. Such limitations on human mental capacity are natural and not subject to correction from the view of this study.

There are similarities between entrepreneurial foresight and general ability. When some ability emerges from education and experience, there is still some element that comes from the luck of birth—being born with genes that assist one intellectually and being born into a family that provides an environment and opportunities for development that are far above the norm. Such factors may be reflected in the managerial and entrepreneurial abilities of individuals, but they are obviously beyond the scope of public policy that affects business. Although it is difficult to identify the factors that are determinants of personal ability, it is clear that these are important ingredients in business success. As such, they constitute an element that this book views as a part of the overall environment of a firm. In society there is a distribution of individuals with certain abilities that exists at any one time. These abilities determine to some extent the success of individual organizations, but they, similar to a constraint placed on all organizations by the government, are assumed not to affect the potential performance of all firms.

Finally, people have personal preference functions. Each person has a different set of goals and desires. Not all persons wish to be in organizations that are striving to grow, or, even if they wish for such prosperity, the desire to achieve it is swamped by a desire for other things, such as leisure or stability. Many persons, especially in small, family-type firms, are satisfied with a certain level of performance or achievement. They may not care to or be willing to take the steps necessary to make the organization grow beyond a certain level. This is not to assume that people who place a higher value on stability are found in family firms; indeed, more may be found in larger organizations. However, their limited desire to achieve growth assures them of a role below the level of top decision makers in the organization, so their personal preferences should not determine the course taken by the organization.

It is not appropriate to say that firm growth is good. That is a value judgment. We observe that most people are interested in the prosperity that generally accompanies or results in growth, but we place no value judgment on those who do not value growth. There is simply no reason to be concerned about such a personal value; the full range of values have a place in the multitude of organizations that exist in a private enterprise economy.

Other factors that may be termed internal natural limits to growth have been identified in other literature and could be expounded here, but the point of this study is not to be concerned with such topics in general. Rather, the study now proceeds to develop factors that can inhibit growth that are beyond the scope of the individual.

4 Natural-External Barriers to Firm Growth

For a variety of reasons, small firms may find growth difficult despite the existence of managerial incentive, ability, and other favorable internal factors. New and small firms desiring to expand in a given industry often face absolute cost and efficiency disadvantages relative to their large, established rivals. These barriers to growth do not result from internal limitations (discussed in chapter 3), artificial-regulatory restraints (discussed in chapter 5), or strategic behavior of market rivals (discussed in chapter 6). They simply exist because size or experience often provides its own reward, a disadvantage to those who have not achieved it. Thus, these factors will be referred to as natural-external limits to growth. In effect, they are what the traditional industrial organization literature would refer to as barriers to entry, although that term is too simplistic to capture the complete essence of these factors.

The traditional approach to the notion of entry barriers asserts that the condition of free entry into industries cannot be met unless established firms have absolute cost advantages over potential entrant firms (Bain 1956). When the concept of entry is broadened to include not only de novo entry but the expansion of the resources administered in existing firms as well (Brozen 1969, p. 11), natural limits to new growth discussed in this section are properly included in the entry barrier classification. According to Stigler, "a barrier to entry may be defined as a cost of producing (at some or every rate of output) which must be borne by a firm which seeks to enter an industry but is not borne by firms already in the industry" (1968, p. 67). These cost (and efficiency) handicaps take a variety of forms, some of which will be quite familiar and commonplace. Other advantages of size and experience are more exotic and the result of rather recent research.

The list of the absolute cost and efficiency advantages associated with being a large or established firm in an industry is long and diverse. However, some order may be imposed by identifying four fundamental types of advantage: technological, pecuniary, temporal, and integrational. Some of these terms are new, or have nontraditional connotations which must be clarified prior to the main discussion of the literature.

Technological advantages of size or scale refer to any factor, phenomenon, or property of production functions that results in falling unit costs as the volume of production increases, all else equal. These result from the more efficient use of labor, materials, and physical capital as a result of size, scale, or experience alone. These may be distinguished from pecuniary advantages of size, scale, or experience that permit large or established firms to acquire inputs at lower dollar outlays. While technological advantages allow larger or established firms to produce goods and services with fewer resources, *pecuniary* advantages allow them to produce goods and services using cheaper resources. Geometrically, pecuniary advantages shift the long-run average cost curve down for the large or established firm, while technological advantages are reflected in the U-shape of such a curve.

Temporal advantages simply refer to the competitive edge enjoyed by firms which have established themselves in markets over time. These include goodwill, firm or market specific capital (know how) with respect to production and distribution, established market and supply contracts, and so forth. In many ways it will be difficult to separate temporal advantages from pecuniary and technological absolute cost advantages. The distinction arises only in the sense that for the latter, a new firm could enjoy them immediately if only it could somehow become large instantaneously. To enjoy the advantages referred to as temporal, a new firm would have to become old instantaneously, which, of course, is impossible.

The final category of cost/efficiency advantage has not yet become an established part of the traditional industrial organization literature. *Integrational* absolute "cost" advantages refer to factors associated with size that increase the firm's ability to rationalize certain failures of the market mechanism. If the firm is defined in terms of suppressing the market mechanism over some range of resource allocation tasks, and if the object of this suppression is to reduce the costs associated with allocating resources via market exchange, then it follows that larger, integrated firms may be more efficient than smaller firms, if size is defined in terms of the number of tasks organized within the firm (Coase 1937). A substantial literature has grown around the notion that purely discrete market transactions often result in inefficiencies known as market or transaction failures (Williamson 1979). Institutional arrangements may be devised to suppress such market transactions in favor of more contractually or organizationally integrated structures. Large vertically or horizontally integrated, or conglomerated, firms will often be better able to resolve these market failures than their smaller nonintegrated rivals. These integrational advantages may place smaller firms at a considerable competitive disadvantage.

The absolute cost and efficiency advantages identified as technological, pecuniary, temporal, and integrational all represent entry barriers that must be considered a fact of life for small firms. Moreover, for the most part, they tend to be nonremediable since eliminating such advantages to large and established firms might require efficiency sacrifices that would serve the interests of smaller firms, but only at a cost to society. This is only true, however, to the extent that large-sized firms offer cost advantages to society. Whenever largeness is due to factors other than superior efficiency, the impact on small firms is a double social loss (Saving 1961; Shepherd 1967).

Technological Advantages of Large-Scale Production

There is good reason to believe that many production processes and market settings lead to a size distribution of firms in which small and large firms coexist in equilibrium (Friedman 1962, p. 142; Stigler 1968, chap. 7; Lucas 1978; Beckenstein 1976). Such a phenomenon is indicative of the fact that small and large firms can both be optimally efficient in a given industrial context because of specialized factors of production, scale economies, and the ability of small firms to fill the "interstices" in the economy left over by their larger competitors. The persistence of both large and small firms in a given industry is also indicative of the fact that there are increasing returns to scale in many production processes which preclude the growth of new, smaller firms once larger, established firms have preempted sufficient market demand. These increasing returns to (or economies of) scale give the latter an absolute cost advantage which limits the growth, if not the survivability, of their smaller rivals. These increasing returns exist whenever a doubling of output does not require a doubling of every productive input (Stigler 1966, p. 153). Most of the explanations of increasing returns are commonplaces of industrial organization theory and will be given only brief mention; others are rather new discoveries and will be discussed in more detail.

One of the earliest discussions of scale economies is found in Smith's *Wealth of Nations* and refers to the increased productivity of human resources when there is a division of labor and specialization of function (1937). The savings of time and motion and the increase in worker dexterity accomplished by labor specialization are, of course, functions of organization size. This is especially true in the division of managerial talent. According to a text on the organization of small firms, one of the disadvantages of small enterprises is the "one-man band" problem: small firms tend to be managed by generalist managers who bear responsibility for a variety of tasks which larger firms assign to specialized managers (Baumback and Lawyer 1979, p. 22). The ability to employ specialized labor requires a planned volume of output which justifies the hiring of specialists and gives larger firms in an industry a natural competitive advantage.

The same applies to the use of physical capital such as specialized machinery. Specialized machines may be designed to produce significant cost savings, but it often occurs that they cannot be scaled down; that is, they are lumpy capital assets. In order for a small firm to enjoy any of the technological advantages of such specialized equipment, it must purchase considerable excess capacity. The costs of this capacity are fixed and must be spread over relatively small volumes of output. As a result, unit costs are necessarily higher for the small scale enterprise. To avoid excess capacity, the small firm would have to forego cost savings associated with specialization. As the enterprise grows, the excess capacity is eliminated. However, unless growth to a scale which allows full utilization of specialized machinery is instantaneous, the small firm always suffers a cost disadvantage relative to larger producers (Scherer 1970, p. 73). Moreover, even when small and large firms employ the same types of general purpose machines, the longer production runs planned by the larger firm gives it a technological advantage. The small firm may employ few such machines and use each to produce a variety of outputs, changing the setup of the machine to produce each variety. The larger firm can assign one machine to each variety of output and avoid considerable setup costs. The high volume firms thus enjoy lower costs and higher productivity per unit of time (Scherer 1970, p. 73).

The general relationship between cost and volume is the subject of a theory of cost of that is directly applicable to the issue at hand. (Alchian 1959). In standard treatments, the unit costs of production are related to the rate of output produced in an efficient production configuration to derive the long run average cost function (Viner 1931; Ferguson 1972, p. 221). The rate of output is only one factor; the contemplated volume of output also has an impact on the unit costs of production, where costs are defined as the sum of discounted future expenditures associated with the planned volume of output. (Alchian 1959, p. 159). For various reasons, for given output rates per unit of time, an increase in the total volume contemplated at the planning stage will decrease average production costs. The relationship between total planned volume and unit costs would appear to be due to better foresight: production may be cheaper when based on a plan to produce some number of units over a long period than it would be when the same number of units are produced by a repetition of short term production plans. But this does not explain the decline in average costs for larger planned volumes. According to Alchian:

> A larger planned (volume) is produced in a different way from that of a smaller planned (volume). . . . The method of production is a function of the volume of output, especially when output is produced from basic dies—and there are few, if any, methods of production that do not involve "dies" (1959, p. 163).

Different production techniques with different costs are best for different volumes of output. Setup costs add more to unit costs at low planned volumes than at higher volumes. Book printing offers the classic example:

once the typesetting has been done, additional copies can be printed at virtually constant marginal costs. Since the making of plates involves a fixed cost, unit costs fall as volume increases. Smaller firms contemplating small volumes thus face higher contemplated unit costs which may serve to frustrate growth plans.

An interesting implication relevant to the question of the entry and growth barriers faced by small firms may be drawn from this relationship between costs and planned volumes of output. Recall that production costs are defined by Alchian as the present value of expected future expenditures. As in all decision making, expectations of the value of key variables affect the allocation of resources. The lower unit costs associated with longer production volumes thus gives larger, established firms what might be termed an expectational absolute cost advantage over smaller, newer firms.

Since the expected life of a new enterprise trying to compete in a market where there are established firms is, historically, shorter than that of firms which have become established, it may be the case that rational small enterprisers plan for lower volume production runs. A firm that is uncertain about its time horizon may choose to produce two units of output over two years using a production plan in the second year that is a repetition of the first year's plan. The entrepreneur could contemplate at the start of the year producing one unit over the period of one year using the best method for such a time and unit volume. At the end of the year he may choose to revise his original plan and produce another unit at the rate of one per year. But it may be cheaper under these circumstances to produce the same two units over two years from a plan for an output of two units to be produced at the rate of one per year, than from a plan to produce two by repetition of methods contemplating only producing one per year for one year (Alchian 1959, p. 163). Thus the unit costs of production for the small new enterprise will be greater than for the larger established firm, *at the planning stage*. This serves to retard the growth orientation mentioned in chapter 1.

This cost is attributable purely to the short time horizon perceived by smaller firms that leads them to adopt less efficient modes of production. This cost disadvantage is remediable to the extent that the small entrepreneur's expectation of life can be extended so as to induce the adoption of larger volume production plans. In contemplating a decision to expand output, one can imagine the existence of a break-even volume of output, given expected demand conditions in the relevant future. This break-even volume will be lower for large planned volumes of output. The new firm in the market whose time horizon is perceived as shorter than those of established firms will need a higher estimate of future demand than the established firms to justify expanding output. Thus, there may be a natural limit to growth contained in the relationship between cost and volume that is simply a function of expectations rather than the physical productivity of inputs, but which will still serve to keep small firms small.

Another source of increasing returns that gives larger firms in the same industry an absolute cost advantage over smaller rivals is found in the workings of the laws of physics. Over some range of sizes, the output of a processing plant (for example, an oil refinery) is roughly proportional to the volume or capacity of the unit, while the resources and construction effort needed to fabricate the facility tend to be proportional to the surface area of the unit's component parts. The area of a three-dimensional structure of constant proportions varies as the two-thirds power of its volume. Given this, the cost of building a processing plant tends to rise less than in proportion to output capacity (Scherer 1970, p. 73; Haldi and Whitcomb 1967). Smaller firms are thus at a cost disadvantage in industries where such a "two-thirds rule" is applicable.

Scale economies also arise due to the operation of the laws of statistics, which have an effect similar in manner to the two-thirds rule. Large firms hold less stock in inventory as a proportion of average sales without having to fear going "out of stock." The demand for a firm's goods is somewhat stochastic, giving rise to the holding of inventories to avoid the losses in sales and goodwill from running out of products. By virtue of the law of large numbers, larger firms may find that the extremes of consumer demand cancel to the mean. As a result, large firms serving many consumers will be able to hold less inventory relative to average final demand, since they are better able to predict average demand. This provides a savings of inventory holding costs that serve as a natural entry barrier, regardless of the underlying nature of the production function. This is an absolute cost advantage of large scale operation.

It has also been suggested that, for similar reasons, scale economies are enjoyed in the holding of cash balances. Firms are required to hold some cash to meet fluctuating payments demands. Such balances have a holding cost since cash does not earn interest; therefore, the firm needs to balance the opportunity cost of holding cash against the benefits of avoiding running short. As in the case of product inventories, larger firms may be able to hold less cash as a percent of average cash outflows than their smaller rivals (Baumol 1952). However, the hypothesis concerning the economies of scale in cash balances still remains to be verified (Brunner and Meltzer 1967).

To the extent that advertising and other promotional activities increase the demand for a firm's product, they are no less factors of production than are the services of a product engineering team or sales staff. As such, one would expect that the production of advertising experiences increasing returns over a range of promotional effort. While the subject of advertising and the limits to new firm growth arises again in the sections on pecuniary cost advantages, artifical strategic barriers to entry, and certain artificial regulatory barriers to growth, there are some purely technological aspects to the relationship between size and costs in the provision of advertising.

First, there are certain fixed costs associated with market research and the physical production of advertising and promotional activities. Whether a firm is large or small, a message must be composed, photos taken, films made, and so forth. Moreover, setting up a distribution system, which may be treated as a form of promotion, involves fixed costs which place a relatively greater burden on smaller firms (Williamson 1963, p. 115). To the extent these costs are spread, the high volume firm has an absolute cost advantage.

Second, up to some level, there are increasing returns to advertising due to the need to expose potential consumers to several messages before their behavior is affected (Scherer 1970, p. 96). One message may have little or no impact on the potential consumer. The maximum effect of advertising may require a saturation level of messages. Telser refers to this as the threshold effect, and large firms with extensive advertising campaigns have an advantage (1964).

Another economy arises in the form of increasing returns because after media exposure, messages are carried by word of mouth. Since the proportion of buyers rises at an increasing rate during the early part of an ad campaign, there may be increasing marginal sales' effectiveness of advertising messages conferring cost advantages on larger advertisers, even without volume discounts (Ozga 1960; Telser 1964, p. 555). These purely technological factors may be treated as natural-external barriers since they convey absolute cost advantages to large firms. Other scale economies associated with advertising are of a pecuniary nature and are discussed in the following section.

Larger size enhances the ability to manage the problem of down-time in production processes. Maintaining uninterrupted production runs is beneficial to the extent that a failure to produce promised output levels reduces goodwill, makes it difficult to fulfill contractual obligations, and wastes other resources while repairs are made. Obtaining the benefits of uninterrupted production is costly. Firms could avoid down-time by purchasing machines of such high quality that they are fail-safe, by maintaining a large repair and maintenance staff to reduce the time a machine is down, or by devoting resources to preventive maintenance efforts. All of these steps might be taken to some degree to establish an optimal trade-off between the costs of down-time and the costs of avoiding such periods of idleness. To the extent that repair and maintenance crews are a fixed cost, large firms may enjoy a technological cost advantage as these costs are spread over larger volumes of output, whatever the chosen level of prevention effort.

Moreover, there are certain "economies of massed reserves" which give larger firms another absolute cost advantage in protecting against production interruptions (E.A.G. Robinson 1958). Insurance against production gaps can be purchased simply by having extra capacity that can be brought on line when mainline equipment fails. Thus, to save costs the speed of repair can be reduced and machines need to be of near perfect quality. For the small firm using few machines, having one idle machine as a back-up represents considerable excess capacity in reserve proportional to total output. For the larger firm with many machines, the same absolute reserve of insurance capacity represents a proportionally smaller level of excess capacity. The larger firm obtains the same amount of protection against interrupted production at lower "carrying cost"—the "economy of massed reserves."

The same applies to the number of repairmen needed to maintain continuous production runs. The number of service personnel required to provide given amounts of service rises less than proportionally to the number of machines which must be serviced (Whitin and Peston 1954). Thus, there are a variety of factors contributing to increasing returns to size in the provision of insurance against equipment breakdowns which place the larger firms in an industry at a competitive advantage.

Economies of massed reserves may extend to the operation of multiplant firms as well (Scherer et al. 1975; Beckenstein 1975, p. 31). A small, single plant firm producing one product will react to demand fluctuations by maintaining inventories and making short-run adjustments in plant utilization. If demand should increase for some reason, the firm simply uses the existing plant more intensively until inventories are replenished. For a normal production function, this will increase the marginal costs of production due to diminishing marginal returns to variable inputs. However, these increases in marginal costs can be reduced for the firm that is large enough to have a number of plants in operation. Local demand increases can be met by shifting production to the lowest marginal cost plant rather than by using the existing plant(s) more intensively. By shipping products from the alternative plant, higher transportation costs will be incurred, but under many circumstances these will be lower than the costs of using the local plant beyond its efficient capacity limit (Scherer 1970, p. 91; A. Manne 1967). Since small firms tend to be single plant firms, the economies of multiplant operation provide an absolute cost advantage to larger competitors.

To summarize, increasing returns give large plants or firms an absolute cost advantage that is not available to smaller rivals. The sources of these scale economies are varied, but all have in common several properties. First, each advantage enjoyed by large-sized firms accrues solely to size rather than differential skill in management. Second, larger firms enjoy these advantages due to the increased productivity of total resources at larger volumes of output produced and marketed. Third, technological scale economies will give larger firms an absolute cost advantage regardless of the unit cost of inputs. There is often simply a more favorable ratio of usable output to input for larger scale operations. Since efficiency is defined in terms of the ratio of usable output to input (Knight 1951, p. 10), technological absolute cost advantages are generally nonremediable limits to new growth. For the small enterprise, the superior efficiency of large rivals in some technological respects is simply a fact of life that can reduce their ability to expand as desired.

Pecuniary Advantages of Large-Scale Production

A firm enjoys a pecuniary economy when the unit prices of its inputs are lower because of its size. Pecuniary economies have been distinguished from technological scale economies on the basis of their overall impact on social costs. For example, Scherer (1970, p. 190) notes that "it is important to distinguish *real* economies of scale, which are realized by making better physical use of labor, materials, and capital inputs, from *pecuniary* economies which result when larger firms pay lower prices for their inputs than smaller firms, e.g., because of superior bargaining power or credit worthiness." Regardless, pecuniary scale economies can adversely affect the ability of new smaller firms to grow in competition with their larger rivals.

An inverse relation between input costs and size is often due to the fact that large units of inputs are really different from smaller units of the same inputs since processing, handling, and packaging costs are less for the former. Moreover, the question of bargaining power is a rather empty issue. Society generally should be indifferent as to who gets the upper hand in a situation of bilateral monopoly. If larger firms have superior bargaining power over smaller suppliers, the social consequences of that power depend on the large firm's market power in the final goods market. If the large firm faces a monopolistic supplier and gets a favorable deal due to size, the advantage will be shared with consumers if there is competition in the final goods market of the large buyer. If, on the other hand, the supplier is competitive, the large firm cannot gain any bargaining advantage due to his larger size without forcing the supplier out of the market. Since, by definition, the small supplier can only earn a competitive return, the large firm simply cannot get a price concession. So superior bargaining power cannot redistribute wealth from a competitive firm to a larger firm; and the same bargaining power may cut into the rents of a smaller monopolistic supplier and either cause those rents to be distributed to consumers where they "should" be or cause a pure transfer from the supplier to the monopolist with no social cost implications whatever. In either case, the cost advantages of large size are real and give larger firms a competitive advantage over smaller rivals that it not necessarily remediable. If superior bargaining power is based upon size, which is in turn based upon technological scales economies, integrational economies, or temporal economies, one cannot eliminate or correct the bargaining power without sacrificing the *real* economies upon which it is founded. Therefore, in this section, pecuniary advantages to large size will be treated as but one species of real economies of scale and considered on an equal basis with the technological, temporal, and integrational varieties.

In general, pecuniary economies of scale or size are manifested in the lower costs of inputs, on a unit basis, paid by large firms in an industry. The focus here is on average rather than marginal costs since in some circumstances it will be the case that small firms will have lower (constant) marginal input costs since they represent such a small part of the total input market. While small firms may be able to purchase all the input it needs at constant cost, the larger firm may have to incur rising marginal input costs for the same percent increase in its output since this represents a much larger absolute increase in input demand. But pecuniary economies always serve to shift the long-run average cost curve for the large scale enterprise below the same function applicable to smaller enterprises. These absolute cost advantages take a variety of forms which apply to virtually all factors of production.

The most obvious pecuniary scale economy accrues to firms that are sufficiently large to buy inputs in large quantities and, hence, receive volume discounts from suppliers (Stigler 1966, p. 153). These discounts do not necessarily represent the outcome of superior bargaining power on the part of large firms. They arise from the fact that shipping, packaging, and handling costs are lower for bulk shipments than they are for job lots. In a sense, the pecuniary economies of scale enjoyed by larger firms are manifestations of increasing returns in the supplying firm that are passed on in a competitive market. The same economies would be enjoyed by the smaller firm if the input was highly durable; the smaller firm could store the input for long periods of time without cost; and interest rates were zero. In such circumstances the small firm could buy a large quantity of the input at a volume discount and use the input over time as needed. Of course, even for durable inputs, the opportunity costs of storage are always positive at positive rates of interest, so small firms cannot enjoy the full pecuniary economies found in volume purchasing. It is just a fact of life that larger producers generally use larger volumes of inputs and can receive the volume discount without incurring the storage costs. Hence, the pecuniary scale economies associated with volume discounts is a natural-external limit to growth faced by smaller firms.

Similar pecuniary economies occur in the advertising and promotion of products. Volume discounts may apply to advertising in the media as well as to the purchase of other conventional inputs. There are certain technological factors contributing to increasing returns in the production of advertising media that may be passed on to quantity purchases of these messages. For example, the per inch cost of print media is less for full page ads than for less-than-page portions. Unit costs may also fall as the geographical area of coverage increases for print and transmission media.

Telser has concluded from his extensive investigation of advertising that the main source of pecuniary scale economies in advertising comes from the rate structure that offers volume discounts to large clients. For example, a large multiproduct firm can have all of its products advertised by the same agency and enjoy certain economies in transaction and setup costs of a fixed nature. In either case there appears to be some a priori reason to expect that large firms enjoy some absolute cost advantages of a pecuniary nature in the promotion of their products.

The provision of financial capital is also subject to volume discounts (not related to risk which is discussed below) because of certain economies in the provision of financial services. First, as with the provision of any input, there are always certain fixed costs which naturally produce lower unit costs at larger output levels. The most important of these are the costs associated with floating new securities issues. The larger the issue, the smaller the transaction cost per dollar raised. This phenomenon has been demonstrated empirically (Archer and Faeber 1966). Similar scale economies are encountered when securing debt capital, but to a lesser degree since less legal assistance is required. Pecuniary economies of this sort will be enjoyed in the acquisition of other inputs which are themselves subject to increasing returns in production. Even where inputs are supplied at constant or increasing costs, there may be pecuniary economies enjoyed by large firms owing to largeness per se. The classic example of such an absolute cost advantage is in the provision of equity capital and involves risk differentials.

Financial capital is produced with decreasing returns to scale since there are rising marginal costs of producing capital, that is, to induce savers to part with their funds. Yet even with constant supply prices of financial capital, large firms can enjoy an absolute cost advantage in acquiring capital because of risk differentials that allow creditors to receive the same utility from a lower accounting return on their investment. That is, because the variance of the return stream (risk) for large firms may be lower than for small enterprises, the cost of equity capital may be lower. Because the risk of ruin is also lower for larger enterprises, the cost of debt capital is similarly lower than for the smaller rivals in the same industry.

The literature relevant to these absolute cost advantages in the capital markets is extensive and somewhat inconclusive. However, the logical foundations of the inverse relationship between risk and firm size is settled because it is a simple matter of statistical regularities. This relationship is based in part on the fact that established firms are less risky because they have established some history of success. This temporal feature is discussed in the next section. Here the discussion focuses solely on the inverse relationship between size of operation and risk to invested or lent capital.

The relative stability of profits, or net returns, earned by large firms can be attributed to several factors. Two specific cases have been suggested. First, large firms generally display greater market power than small firms and, hence, are better able to stabilize earnings. The lower costs of financial capital may be used by the larger firm to increase its hold on the market to the disadvantage of its smaller rivals. Second, the ability to spread risks increases with the size of the firm (Scherer 1970, p. 101). The inverse relationship between monopoly power and return variance may be correct, as Scherer suggests, but this may have little to do with the conscious use of market power "to stabilize earnings." The relationship may simply be a matter of statistical law rather than the volition of monopolists.

Demand for any given product is stochastic. In such a stochastic demand environment a seller does not know exactly how much output will be taken in the market at a particular price. However, he may know the parameters of the probability distribution of demand. A general specification for such a stochastic demand function would be:

$$D^e = f^e (V, p, u_1, u_2, u_3, a^e)$$

where D^e is the firm's estimate of demand per time period, V is a vector of information variables used to predict demand, p is the unit price of the good, and u_1, u_2, and u_3 are the random components of firm, industry, and aggregate demand respectively (Gordon and Hynes 1970, p. 383). The inverse relationship between return variance and monopoly power may be deduced from the extreme case of pure monopoly.

For the pure monopolist the random component of firm and industry demand are the same, since the firm is the industry. Firms with less than 100 percent market-share must be concerned with relative market-share as well as the random components of industry and aggregate demand. For smaller firms the loss (or gain) of a given number of customers will have relatively more impact on overall demand variance than for a larger firm. Hence, an inverse relationship between risk, measured in terms of demand and profit variance, and firm size may be transmitted via the relationship between firm size and market share. This may result in a nonremediable barrier to growth. The second group of factors leading to the decline of return variance with size include the statistical law of large numbers, the insurance principle, and the portfolio theory.

Taking the latter first, to the extent that larger firms tend to engage in product diversification, they can reduce return variance by intelligently diversifying their "portfolio" of products in the final goods market. The classic heuristic example here is that of the producer of raincoats who takes on the production of suntan lotion to insure against the vagaries of the weather. This type of conglomerative activity converts two high variance return streams into an enterprise return stream with lower observed variance due to the inverse correlation between the demand for raincoats and suntan lotion. This result is a commonplace of investment portfolio theory (Sharpe 1970). All else equal, the ability to diversify product lines in such a manner is an increasing function of overall enterprise size and, hence, gives larger firms an absolute advantage in risk reduction over their smaller rivals. However, diversification is not the only factor responsible for the predicted inverse relationships between size and return variance. Even single-product large firms may have an absolute advantage in this regard.

In his classic treatise, *Risk, Uncertainty, and Profit*, Knight focused upon methods undertaken by entrepreneurs to reduce the uncertainties involved in producing goods for general markets. Knight saw two possibilities for reducing uncertainty. The uncertainties associated with the production of goods and service over time are less in groups than in single cases (Knight 1971, p. 238). That is, it is easier to achieve greater accuracy in predicting the mean of some random variable over a larger number of cases than over a smaller number. For longer production runs or larger final goods markets, the extremes of cost or demand behavior tend to cancel to the mean. This ability to reduce business uncertainty through the consolidation of cases "constitutes a strong incentive to extend the scale of operations of a business establishment (since) . . . there is a greater probability that bad guesses will be offset by good ones and that a degree of constancy and dependability in the total results will be achieved" (Knight 1971, p. 252). Thus, not only is it easier to estimate the values of key profit-related variables over larger volumes of output and larger markets, but also when mistakes occur, as they will, the overall impact on the enterprise will be less severe in larger firms than in their smaller rivals. This clearly suggests that when firms get larger, they enjoy a risk advantage over their smaller rivals whose growth may be thwarted.

Moreover, the large scale enterprise is likely to be financed by a large number of individuals, each contributing a modest portion of the total capitalization of the firm. According to Knight, this diffuses risk. Each person in the large enterprise faces a relatively smaller exposure to the hazards of untoward contingencies. As Knight (1971, p. 239) observes, when all else is equal, "It is a gain to have an event cause a loss of a thousand dollars each to a hundred persons rather than a hundred thousand dollars to one person," all else equal. Consolidating risk, and diffusing it, lowers the return variance for the business enterprise. Since larger firms are more effective in this, there is a logically based inverse relationship between size and riskiness. The inverse relationship translates into an absolute pecuniary cost advantage for the large enterprise.

Much of the impact of lower risk on the cost of capital is because of human nature. There are three basic attitudes among people toward risk which may be identified. These are the risk seeking, risk aversion, and risk neutrality attitudes. The risk seeker will prefer an investment that has the same expected return as any other investment but with a greater variance. The risk averter will choose an investment that offers the same expected return as others but lower variance. The risk neutral peson is simply indifferent: as long as the expected monetary return from two investments is the same, the variance of return is irrelevant. While persons of all persuasions exist in the investment community, both reason and empirical research suggest that most investors are risk averse (Pappas and Brigham 1979, p. 83). Risk aversion follows from the principle of diminishing marginal utility applied to money.

On an a priori basis, it is reasonable to assume that money, like all goods, is subject to diminishing personal rates of substitution as the amount a person holds increases, ceteris paribus. That is, the marginal utility of an extra dollar is less when you are holding ten dollars than when you are holding five dollars. The impact of this principle on risk aversion is straightforward. Given the diminishing marginal utility of money, and the same initial position, the pleasure from a dollar gained is always less than the pain associated with a dollar lost, given the same initial position. Risk means that there is some probability that the actual return on an investment will be less than expected. Of course it could be more, but the adverse impact on the investor's utility associated with the failed expectation is greater than the favorable impact on utility of an expectation that is exceeded. The bottom line is the requirement that for a risk averse investor to be indifferent to two investments, the one with the greater risk must also offer the greatest expected return. Knight (1971, p. 236) provides the common sense of the matter: "If a man is undergoing a sacrifice for the sake of a future benefit, the expected reward must be larger in order to evoke the sacrifice if it is viewed as contingent than if it is considered certain, and that it will have to be larger in at least some general proportion to the degree of felt uncertainty in the anticipation." Since, as indicated, there is some reason to believe that larger firms have greater opportunities for reducing return variance, it follows that they should be able to attract financial capital at lower money costs than smaller firms.

A priori, larger firms should have an absolute pecuniary advantage over their smaller rivals in the capital-input markets with respect both to debt and equity (Brigham and Smith 1967; Scherer 1970, pp. 100-102). While the logic of an inverse relationship between size and the cost of capital is straightforward, empirical verification of the hypothesis is far from settled. The issue, of course, center on the relative costs of capital faced by small firms and large firms, all else equal. Several studies suggest an absolute cost advantage to size along the lines suggested by a priori reasoning (Alexander 1949; Samuels and Smythe 1968; Alberts and Archer 1973; Steckler 1964).

With respect to the impact of diversification on return variance and, hence, capital costs, Scherer concludes that the conjecture that diversified firms experience low return variance has not been supported, perhaps because the pure conglomerate is a creature of theory with no real world counterpart (1970, p. 102). Moreover, it may very well be the case that since stockholders can diversify through portfolio selection, the marginal gains to internal diversification, as reflected in the ex post performance of conglomerates, will naturally be unimpressive. Despite the lack of conclusive empirical evidence, there can be no question that on the basis of logic alone, risk spreading through product and market diversification conveys some advantage upon the large firm able to engage in such activity and must be counted among the potential natural-external barriers faced by smaller enterprises.

The evidence with respect to cost differentials in raising equity capital is also unsettled but only because of certain measurement problems. Alberts and Archer (1973) find that the cost of raising outside equity is lower for larger corporations than for small corporations (abstracting from flotation costs, which are less for larger firms for reasons already discussed). This relationship is inferred from the finding of an inverse relationship between the size of a corporation (appropriately defined) and the variance in the corporations's rate-of-return (also appropriately defined). Like other studies of this kind, two presumptions provide the basis for the analysis.

First, it is assumed that the ex ante riskiness assigned by investors to a particular security is a function of the historical variability of the company's rate-of-return. Second, it is assumed that there is some component of any firm's rate-of-return which represents the risk free element plus a risk premium. Hence, the inverse relationship between size and the cost of capital is a manifestation of an inverse relationship between historical return variance and the actual risk premium assigned, ex ante, to a given firm's securities. However, it is simply not an established fact that ex post rate of return variability is a reliable surrogate for the riskiness *perceived* by the investors making investment decisions, nor is it established that the ex ante risk perceived necessarily results in a risk premium. (Goudzwaard 1973, p. 243).

To establish a genuine inverse relationship between the cost of capital

and firm size, it is necessary to establish that investors require a risk
premium when investing in smaller enterprises because they believe that
these firms are inherently more risky. But can this be inferred from the simple fact that ex post returns variance is higher for smaller firms? There are
many reasons why smaller firms will not return as much to investors as
larger firms, and these could result in risk premiums independent of
historical return variance. It is not that there is reason to believe that the
hypothesized inverse relationship between size and the cost of capital does
not exist; it is just that some prefer a more direct measure of the cost of
capital in empirical work. As Alberts and Archer noted with respect to their
own empirical work: "Suppose that what we are seeing . . . is primarily the
impact of a tendency for smaller companies to be distributed more heavily
than larger companies in industries subject to unstable demand
conditions." (1973). Hence, the use of ex post return variance in empirical
work would simply capture inter-industry risk differentials rather than large
firm-small firm differentials. Regardless, the logic of the capital market
clearly suggests that smaller firms face an absolute pecuniary cost disadvantage in raising investment funds; empirical validation of this hypothesis remains to be accomplished.

Another possibility explored in the literature involves the possible existence of an equity gap that places small firms at a disadvantage in the equity capital market even in the absence of genuine differences in ex post return
variability. An equity gap exists if capital resources are more costly for
small firms than for larger firms in the same risk class (measured appropriately), when one abstracts from differences in managerial ability and
flotation costs. The existence of such a gap would reflect either the existence
of capital rationing on the part of lenders favoring large corporations for
reasons not directly related to economic considerations or "a systematic
overestimate or risk and/or underestimate of return for small firms on the
part of the public" (Stoll and Curley 1970, p. 310). However, Stoll and
Curley found no evidence of an equity gap, so defined.

They found, in fact, that investors seem to be eager to invest in small
firms; and that, if anything, too much capital is devoted to the issues of
smaller enterprise relative to some standard of economic rationality. One
explanation offered is that the typical investor in small issues is a highflyer
(risk seeker) or that there is some form of capital rationing in reverse. That
is, some people prefer to invest in small firms for reasons unrelated to
economic considerations. Thus, this study does not refute the contention
that differences in the cost of capital among small and large firms are simply a matter of differences in expected return variance, as indicated above.
Such a difference represents a pecuniary absolute cost advantage to size
and, hence, a natural-external limit to new growth for smaller enterprises.
Moreover, such a limit must for the most part be considered a
nonremediable limit to growth since it is based upon the law of statistics.

Temporal Absolute Advantages of Size

To this point a number of natural barriers to the ability of small firms to grow and develop in competition with larger rivals have been identified. In addition to these factors the new small firm faces difficulties which have less to do with asset size, the rate of output, or the quantity of inputs purchased than with the fact that new firms have been around for less time than their established rivals. The purpose of this section is to discuss the advantages accruing to firms that have established themselves in markets prior to subsequent potential entrants. The fact that in most cases new entrants tend to be smaller than established firms is not a factor here. Temporal advantages refer to the historical age of the organization rather than other structural features such as size. However, since firms may fail to grow because of temporal barriers, size and newness may be correlated.

One of the primary advantages of being established is the existence of a strong and stable preference pattern for the firm's output among its customers (Williamson 1963, p. 113). In fact, product differentiation is considered one of the primary barriers to entry in the traditional industrial organization literature (Bain 1956, p. 142). The use of advertising expenditures to bar the entry of new rivals is discussed later. The ability to differentiate one's product and, hence, establish consumer loyalty is an important function of advertising expenses and the increasing returns to advertising. However, the time factor is also important. As Telser notes, in promotional activity, "there might be a threshold of awareness such that consumers fail to notice a product unless they have received at least a certain number of messages" (1964, p. 555). This phenomenon may result from a certain amount of inertia on the part of consumer that places a premium on being an established advertiser.

A firm that has devoted efforts to promotion has established goodwill and an association between brand name and the function of the product. To accomplish the same level of consumer recognition, the new firm would have to produce many more messages over the short run. As a result, short-run marginal costs of production would be greater for the new firm due to diminishing marginal returns to the promotional effort. Maintaining customer loyalty may be cheaper than establishing such loyalty over short periods. This gives established firms a short-term temporal advantage over newer rivals. That is, many of the beneficial effects of advertising are cumulative in nature; as a result, the marginal efficiency of advertising efforts increases with the passage of time alone. This effect applies even to minimal amounts of advertising. Therefore, in this respect time is a natural barrier to entry operating through advertising, not solely a strategic or artificial barrier as often claimed.

Another major advantage accruing to established firms in an industry stems from the phenomenon of learning by doing (Alchian 1959; Stigler

1966, pp. 171-74). Although much emphasis is placed upon the importance of organized scientific research, many innovations in the process of producing things (as well as distributing them) may come from the person on the spot. Knowledge of particular circumstances of time and place, or know-how, cannot be obtained by organized research efforts, but comes from experience and represents a very important type of knowledge in decentralized processes (Hayek 1945, p. 521). Adam Smith once observed that "a great part of the machines made use of in those manufacturers in which labor is most subdivided, were originally the inventions of common workmen, who, being each of them employed in some very simple operation, naturally turned their thoughts toward finding out easier and readier methods of performing it" (Smith 1937, bk. I, chap. 1). To the extent that this applies to the design of distribution systems, personnel practices, materials handling, and so forth, older firms will have a natural edge over inexperienced rivals. This phenomenon contributes to the predicted fall in unit costs as a function of volume discussed previously (Alchian 1959). Inexperience is a classical natural limit to new growth, taking the form of a temporal cost disadvantage.

Other absolute cost advantages enjoyed by established firms involve the capture of unique, scarce resources. Having entered the market first, established firms are likely to have found the best locations for plants with respect to potential markets and sources of supply. In addition, they will have found the cheapest sources of raw materials, including skilled labor (Johns 1962, p. 49). As long as the long-run supply function for these resources is upward sloping, established firms will face lower production costs simply by virtue of their early arrival on the scene. The new firm cannot capture such advantages by better management, larger scale operation, or cheaper source of capital. Such advantages which accrue to established firms through their early access to superior sources of supply or market location are natural barriers to new growth.

Established firms also may have an advantage over newer rivals through the lower costs they must pay inputs, especially those involving firm-specific capital investments (human or financial). For example, new firms may find it difficult to attract some types of skilled labor because greater uncertainty is associated with employment in new ventures. In order for them to be induced to engage in the development of specialized skills, human agents must have some assurance that the investment costs will be amortized over a number of periods of employment. Like other forms of investment activity, investing in human capital involves a fixed cost. Moreover, human agents tend to treat investments in themselves in a manner similar to the treatment of financial investment decisions (Becker 1975). The established firm offers an implicit guarantee that human capital expenditures will be rewarded over time. The risk of losing employment for reasons other than lack of performance by an employee is less in the established enterprise than it is in the new firm, all else equal. As a result, the same utility of employment can be offered a worker at a lower monetary wage in the established firm. Because it is riskier to the skilled employee, the new firm may have to offer higher monetary rewards to labor, thus, placing itself at a competitive disadvantage.

New firms face similar temporal disadvantages in raising financial capital. The risk of ruin and the return variance applicable to a given firm's bonds or equities are not known with certainty at the time of investment. These key variables must be estimated, and such estimation requires information. Some information is provided by the past performance of the firm's decision makers. Since newer firms have shorter histories than established firms, investors must make estimates of expected risk based upon less information. Under such circumstances, rational investors will use low cost proxies for needed information (Akerlof 1970, p. 488; Spence, 1971). Factors such as product type, business-cycle sensitivity, labor intensiveness, and so forth may be used. Where detailed information is absent, firms may be lumped into groups based upon such factors. This necessary and rational behavior on the part of investors can work to the disadvantage of newer firms.

Newer firms can be either good or poor investment risks depending upon the quality of management, firm specific capital, labor force skills, and so forth. When investors rely upon information proxies, new firms that will, in fact, be high quality, because of their limited history, may be lumped together with new firms that will be low quality. The high quality newer firms would like to be differentiated from the low quality new firms in the same general category but cannot where information is imperfect. Established high quality firms do not have this problem, at least to the same extent, because of the information content in their history. As a result, older high quality firms may be able to raise capital at a lower risk premium than high quality new firms, simply due to the availability of information. This is a temporal barrier to new growth. Capital costs may be lower for the established firm that is exactly the same as the new firm in every respect but age. This natural limit to the growth of new firms is remediable only to the extent that information which simply does not exist can be made to exist—that is, by magic. Hence, it is but one of the many facts of life which place new, and generally smaller, firms at a temporal absolute cost disadvantage with respect to their established, and generally larger, rivals.

Integrational Advantages Associated with Large-Scale Operation

The essence of economic integration is the suppression of the market mechanism as a mode of organizing production and exchange. Individuals will choose to suppress the price mechanism, or market exchange, as a mode of interaction whenever the costs of using the price mechanism compare unfavorably with the costs associated with alternate means of allocating resources. This transaction cost approach to industrial organization theory made its first appearance in Coase's seminal article, "The Nature of the Firm" (1937). He reasoned that resources will be administered within firms whenever the cost of negotiating contracts in markets exceeded the rising costs of internal administration due to scale diseconomies. The success of the business firm as a method of organizing production among numerous suppliers of human and other resources stands as testimony to the advantages of integration: the firm is the archetypal example of suppressing the market mechanism. To the extent that larger firms more extensively suppress the price mechanism in organizing production, they stand to enjoy certain absolute efficiencies and, hence, cost advantages over their smaller, less integrated rivals. Such advantages translate into what will be called integrational limits to new growth. The integrated firm gains an advantage over its nonintegrated rivals not only from sheer size but also from the advantages of being able to avoid certain failures of the market mechanism which retard overall economic efficiency. Some of these advantages are commonplaces of traditional industrial organization theory and will be discussed later in this section.

Other advantages may be inferred from a rather new body of research known as transactions-cost economics (Williamson 1979). One of the principle advantages of large integrated firms lies in the fact that a variety of costs or other disadvantages associated with market transactions are eliminated when exchange takes place across divisions via memos rather than among firms via contracts. The avoidance of sales taxes is only the most obvious aspect of such an advantage. Other aspects include the ability to avoid the distortions of monopoly supply and public price regulations (Stigler 1968, p. 136).

Of perhaps more significance is the fact that integration allows the more effective husbanding of proprietary information. For example, if a small firm engages in research and development activity and invents what is believed to be a salable product or efficient production process, it will probably have to go into the capital markets for funds. In the process it will have to divulge information about the project to potential creditors. That information may leak out as a result, to the disadvantage of the smaller firm (Mueller 1972). Larger firms are such that the R&D division may only have to convince its own finance people of the idea's value and keep the information inside the firm. This provides an improved flow of information and capital within the larger firm (Mueller 1972, p. 201). These firms can use retained earnings to finance themselves. Since the provision of capital within an organization rather than through the capital markets clearly is a suppression of market mechanisms, such advantages that accrue to larger firms in this regard are properly categorized as integrational.

Another integrational advantage accruing to the larger firms involves the efficient flow of managerial talent to its highest valued uses. It has been suggested that it may be quicker to replace an inefficient division manager within an integrated firm by administrative decision than to replace the manager of such a division if the organization were owned by the manager (Alchian 1969, p. 349). That is, the internal personnel "market" within integrated firms may be more efficient than the external open market for managers. The same applies to other types of labor and gives the larger firm a potential integrational advantage over smaller rivals.

The same reasoning applies to the external versus internal capital markets. Once again the investment funds market within a larger integrated corporation may allocate funds within the organization with greater speed and accuracy than the external organized capital market (Alchian 1969, p. 349). If one treats the divisions within a firm as quasi-market participants, it is clear that information may flow more rapidly with the organization than between a given producer and the impersonal capital market. Here it is not the ability to keep information within the firm that conveys the advantage, but the ability to overcome the problems of accurately communicating information between nonintegrated entities, which places less integrated firms at a disadvantage in the allocation process. To the extent that size and multidivisioned organizations are positively correlated, large firms will enjoy advantages not open to smaller rivals.

Integrated firms enjoy an advantage over their nonintegrated rivals in the supply of other resources besides managerial talent, skilled labor, and capital. Backward vertical integration (incorporating a source of supply within the organization) is also advantageous, principally for two reasons. First, owing the source of supply allows integrated firms to avoid the adverse effects of monopoly or cartel pricing of raw materials (Scherer 1970, p. 87). Second, the vertically integrated firm is able to avoid production interruptions due to rationing or other breakdowns in supply channels which may occur when the source of supply is owned by another entity. Moreover, the firm that integrates forward into distribution can gain tremendous absolute efficiency and marketing advantages over rivals limiting themselves to manufacturing alone. For example, new car customers may be more willing to buy a car from an integrated auto producer since they know they can obtain service from an authorized company dealer. As Scherer (1970, p. 57) notes, "Establishing . . . a network (of dealers) is difficult for the smaller manufacturer since there are economies of scale at the sales and service establishment level."

In addition, the vertically integrated firm can avoid the problems arising from what is called opportunistic behavior that may occur when suppliers and manufacturers are linked only through the price mechanism. The new transaction-cost approach to economic analysis suggests that integration makes firms more efficient in that it allows certain technologically efficient configurations of production to take place which might never occur if transactions were organized only through simple market exchange (Klein et al. 1978; Williamson 1971, 1979; Liebeler 1979).

Vertical integration of production commonly is taken to be advantageous for technological reasons or for economizing on the costs of using the market. But Williamson has noted that "in more numerous respects than are commonly appreciated, the substitution of internal organization for market exchange is attractive less on account of technological economies associated with production but because of what may be referred to as 'transactional failures' in the operation of markets for intermediate goods" (1971, p. 112). Advantages of integration with respect to the resolution of transactional (market) failures exist for both forward and backward integration. The theory is best illustrated by reference to examples.

The classic example of the technological advantages of vertical integration involves the merging of ingot casting and component shaping in the steel industry into a continuous operation. It is common to treat the cost saving associated with not having to reheat the steel at later stages of the production process as the main integrational advantage. But this advantage, being purely technological, need not produce any demand for suppressing the price mechanism. The ingot firm and the fabricating firm could deal with each other through day to day contracts and enjoy all the technological advantages of integration simply by locating their plants in close physical proximity to each other. The demand for some type of legal or ownership integration arises from the fact that this physical integration may not be adequate to avoid all the costs of relying on the price mechanism to organize exchange.

One situation where the suppression of the market mechanism will be advantageous arises when there is "an opportunity for the parties to a transaction to take advantage of each other in circumstances in which the other's next best alternatives are significantly less advantageous" (Liebeler 1979, p. 29). Such a circumstance would arise were two individuals to build an ingot plant and a fabricating plant which were only physically integrated. Once the physical capital is in place, the next best market alternative for the ingot producer vis-à-vis the physically close fabricator is rather poor, and vice versa. That is, each could take advantage of the other with respect to the prices charged for their respective products because viable competitors are absent. As a result, the transfer price of hot ingot is subject to bargaining with a range set by the next best alternatives of each party. The ingot producer cannot extract more from the fabricator for his ingot than the market price of comparable (cold) ingot delivered to the fabricator's plant (plus reheating costs); the fabricator, on the other hand, cannot force the ingot producer to accept less than the return from marketing cold iron to the closest alternative fabricator. Given this range of potential dispute, considerable savings in transactions costs may be achieved by simply integrating the plants legally, through contract or merger. Without such an ownership integration, it may not be feasible to enjoy the technological cost advantages.

For example, under the uncertainty induced by potential opportunistic behavior, nonintegrated firms might hold greater than optimum inventories relative to the appropriate level (with respect to capacity) under certainty. In addition, the cost of negotiating transfer prices are eliminated under the integrated mode of organization (Klein et al. 1978, p. 301). But more importantly, without some form of vertical integration, given the possibility of opportunistic behavior, the technological efficiencies of production may never materialize. Without some means of dealing with this opportunism phenomenon, in the extreme, no plants may be built at all. Thus, the transactional advantages of integration confer an absolute cost advantage on the integrated firm relative to its nonintegrated rivals, and permit them to attain certain scale economies which might not be possible without some form of integration.

The primary alternative to vertical integration as a solution to the general problem of opportunistic behavior is some form of economically enforceable long-term contract. Unfortunately, such contracts have been treated as per se violations of the Sherman Act in the past, and this tends to foreclose smaller, nonintegrated firms from the considerable advantages of integration through contract (Klein et al. 1978, p. 302). This is a regulatory restraint on new growth that will be discussed in chapter 5.

Forward vertical integration also allows firms to avoid certain transaction failures which plague firms that rely upon the price mechanism to organize exchange between the manufacturing and retailing levels of distribution. Production involves more than the simple manufacture of a product. It also involves the distribution of the product to the ultimate consumer. The provision of an optimal level of local sales effort may be difficult for the nonintegrated manufacturer to organize due to another form of opportunistic behavior that may occur at the retail level. When such a transaction failure arises, the enterprise integrating forward into distribution may enjoy an absolute efficiency advantage over its nonintegrated rivals. The distribution of beer offers a convenient real world example.

A certain brand of beer is produced in such a way that, for maximum quality, it must be kept refrigerated constantly before consumption. For the distributor of this beer, the production of local service effort is a costly activity: special storage facilities must be installed, refrigerated trucks must be maintained, and so on. While distributing a high quality product benefits the distributor, avoiding these costs is also beneficial. Suppose that several independent distributors were permitted to distribute this product produced by a nonintegrated brewer in a given geographical area. Each distributor may sell his beer at a slightly lower price than his rivals by cutting quality (for example, providing a suboptimal amount of refrigeration). Consumers could not tell before buying the beer whether or not the proper amount refrigeration had been provided; and it would be difficult, if not impossible, to tell whether the poor taste was due to the producer, the distributor, or a retailer along the supply chain. Poor quality would reduce the demand for the beer and this would hurt the sales of the guilty distributor. However, the harm would be shared by the manufacturer and other distributors as well. The cheating distributor can try to take advantage of the efforts of other distributors and retailers of the beer to maintain quality.

Since the benefits (increased demand) of providing optimal local service efforts are shared by the cheater and everyone else involved in the total production effort of the beer, no one will have the incentive to produce the optimal level of quality. As a result, the manufacturer loses customers because the high quality beer he produced fails to reach the customer in the same shape that it left the factory. This transactional failure may be resolved through forward vertical integration. Eliminating, through contract or merger, the economic independence of distributors is the integrational option open to the manufacturer. When the organization is hurt by cheating, integration will eliminate spillover effects, and the optimal production of service will take place (Liebeler 1979, p. 36). This absolute efficiency advantage for integrated firms may be explained rather easily.

Advantages of vertical (and in some cases horizontal) integration exist for many products where local sales effort is an important component of the entire production process (Bork 1978, chap. 14). For example, the production of furniture may include hiring a well informed sales staff at the retail level and holding a large inventory to aid consumer choice. Another retailer of the same line of furniture in the same geographical area may attempt to free ride off the high quality retailer by maintaining a skeleton crew of sales people and limited inventory. Customers can shop at the high quality merchant, gather valuable information that is costly to produce, and then buy from the "cheater" at the lower price he can charge since his costs are lower. If the manufacturer owned all its retail outlets, it could divide a geographical area into exclusive divisional territories and avoid the problem. That is, no distributor-division could effectively cheat since it would only hurt itself: the loss of consumers due to poor quality is limited to the distributor responsible since that is the only representative of the manufacturer consumers have contact with. This gives an absolute advantage to the integrated firm.

Of course smaller manufacturers might try to integrate contractually by engaging in territorial marketing agreements with distributors. This would solve the free-rider problem identified above, but, unfortunately for the smaller enterprises tempted to try this form of contract integration, antitrust officials have considered this behavior anticompetitive. Once again, this is a regulatory impediment to the success of small firms which will be discussed in chapter 5.

To summarize, larger firms in a given industry may enjoy a natural advantage over their smaller rivals to the extent that they are able to exploit the several advantages of suppressing the price mechanism in organizing exchange. In the provision of labor inputs and capital, and in the husbanding of proprietary information, avoiding the market mechanism provides absolute cost and efficiency advantages to the larger integrated firms not available to newer and smaller rivals. Smaller firms operating in fewer levels of the production process are also less able to avoid certain transaction failures which may only be resolved by suppressing market exchange across various distribution levels. Since the smaller firms are usually nonintegrated, integrational advantages provide a final example of the natural limits to the growth of small firms which take the form of absolute cost and efficiency advantages of scale.

Summary

The absolute cost and efficiency advantages which accrue to larger firms in most cases must be treated by the small firm and the policy maker as a fact of life. Many of these advantages are a function of large scale operation, size itself, or experience, and are not remediable without losing considerable, productive efficiencies. As Stigler has observed, "An efficient size firm . . . is one that meets any and all problems the entrepreneur actually faces: strained labor relations, rapid innovation, government regulation, unstable foreign markets, and what not" (1968, p. 73). This chapter has provided a synthesis of the relevant industrial organization literature with an emphasis on Stigler's "what not" category, that is, nontraditional treatments of the absolute cost and efficiency advantages of large and established firms. Greater efficiency, either productive or transactional, will inevitably limit the growth and success of new and potential entrants in a given market. As such they have been classified as natural-external barriers to new growth to distinguish them from artificial barriers, resulting from the predatory and anticompetitive intentions of large firms and the inadvertant by-products of regulatory activity. Those limits to new growth are the topics of the next two chapters.

5 Artificial-Regulatory Barriers to Firm Growth

The factors limiting the growth and development of new or small firms discussed to this point for the most part have been limited to purely private market behavior. Many of these factors involve structural attributes of smallness which place these firms at an absolute cost disadvantage with respect to larger rivals in the same industry. Among these are the inherent riskiness of small enterprises that contributes to high mortality, the absence of a track record which inhibits the ability to attract debt financing, the high costs of equity capital due to high ex ante estimates of the risks facing small enterprise, a lack of managerial talent, the inability to exploit scale economices in production, and so forth. In addition, large firms may engage in strategic behavior which serves to retard the growth of smaller rivals. These limits to new growth include traditional barriers to entry and certain exclusionary practices such as building excess capacity, limit pricing, and selective price cutting intended to foreclose competition.

In addition to these structural and strategic limits to the successful development of small enterprise, the literature reveals that many of the difficulties faced by small business arise as an inadvertent by-product of public policies, the direct objectives of which are far removed from the small business area. The purpose of this chapter is to discuss these external barriers to new growth. They are called artificial in that they are the artifacts of human design. They are not the result of any human intention to place roadblocks in the way of new, growing enterprises. However, they may be no less effective as a barrier to growth because of this.

In the following discussion of regulatory problems, it must be remembered that the policies to be discussed here presumably do have beneficial social functions. However, without some estimate of the adverse impact these policies have on other sectors, such as the small business community, policy formation very easily can stray from certain efficiency norms. Specifically, where policy is made without due consideration of fully reckoned costs, regardless of whether those costs are rather indirect, attainment of social optima will not be possible. Therefore, an investigation of the inadvertent effects of various government policies and programs on small business potentially is beneficial to society at large as well as to small business in particular. Moreover, of all the barriers to small firm growth discussed, these are potentially the most remediable. Unlike many of the structural and, to a lesser extent, strategic limits to new growth, which often represent the facts of life for small enterprise, each of these barriers may be eliminated or modified as they were created: by conscious design. That is, these limits to growth are amenable to correction once their impacts are clearly identified.

The nature of the barriers to new growth discussed in this chapter is best illustrated in the enactment and enforcement of federal and state securities regulation. The purpose of these laws is to promote capital formation in the economy by providing protections for investors from unscrupulous issuers of equity shares. Such protection was believed to increase investor confidence and, hence, enhance the ability of firms to attract capital from the equity market. Thus, the objective of the policy represented by the federal and state securities laws was to promote capital formation by protecting investors. Unfortunately, there may be reason to suspect that these goals are incompatible to some extent. This indirect limit to the growth of small firms will be discussed in detail later. First, several other such artificial barriers suggested by the literature will be outlined.

Social Legislation and Regulation
as a Regressive Tax on Small Business

A broad range of social policies are designed to promote the interests of a variety of groups in society and achieve other desirable ends. Protection of the poor from low wages and high rates of interest, protection of those who depend upon pensions for their incomes, protection of workers and consumer from the hazards of the work place, protection of the environment, and protection of the rights of minorities are objects of various social policies in the United States. Regardless of the ability of policies to meet their objectives, it may be the case that the costs they impose on business in general are borne more intensely by small business in particular (Joint Economic Committee 1978). Thus, Narver and Preston (1976, p. 20) argue that "there is increasing evidence that public policy in general, and federal regulatory activity in particular, places extraordinarily heavy burdens on the smaller enterprises and, indeed, may in many cases be totally inimical to its continued existence." Several attributes of small enterprise may contribute to an explanation of this phenomenon.

First, smaller firms tend to be more labor-intensive than their larger counterparts. When this is the case, changes in labor cost imposed by social legislation will tend to have a more severe impact on small business. The minimum wage law, regulations issued by Occupational Safety and Health Administration, new federal controlling pensions law (ERISA), and equal employment opportunity mandates all have the effect of raising labor costs in one way or another. There is no a priori reason to expect that the per employee costs associated with these policies will differ between large and small firms (although that, itself, is a testable hypothesis); but even with constant per employee costs, the impact of these laws will be relatively greater for firms where the labor component of production costs is significant. For example, in 1978 the unemployment rate for teenagers was 17.3 percent (compared with 6.2 pecent for all workers). Thus, "it is the unskilled, teenage workers, *and the smaller businesses that would normally hire them* as apprentices and trainees, who are most seriously affected when statutory hourly minimum wage rates are increased" (Baumback and Lawyer 1979, p. 23; emphasis added).

Second, since a greater portion of small firms engage in retail activities, the recent surge in consumer activism may tend to impose heavier burdens on these enterprises than on their larger rivals (Narver and Preston 1976, p. 20). As Baumback and Lawyer note, "The impact of the 'new consumerism' is particularly felt at the retail level . . . Nader inspired changes such as unit pricing and open code dating, for example, are bothersome and tend to increase the retailers' costs" (1979, p. 31).

In addition, since dealing with consumer complaints involves a certain fixed investment (for example, consumer complaint department), large firms may enjoy certain scale advantages even if they face the same number of complaints per customer. Regardless of the merits of the consumer protection movement as social legislation, its impact on smaller firms may be more severe than on large firms. However, there is no empirical verification of this hypothesis. The same problems apply to the general administrative burden of regulation (Benston 1977).

Third, there may be absolute size considerations making the impact of well intended environmental protection effort heavier for small firms. If there are scale economies associated with the physical equipment used in pollution control, smaller firms may find themselves in a position of either violating the EPA Regulations or holding excess pollution control capacity. Where pollution control devices represent "lumpy" investments, larger firms will be better able to achieve optimal physical configurations in their cleanup efforts. To the extent that small firms, by virtue of their smallness, are able to escape detections for violating EPA rules, this effect is offset. Therefore the net adverse impact of complying with environmental protection laws vis-à-vis big business is an empirical question that has not yet been addressed in a comprehensive study.

Finally, there are miscellaneous examples of legislation which could have significant though indirect adverse impacts on small business. These are the ERISA legislation, state usury laws, and investment incentives. Pension managers may be more reluctant to invest in high risk securities under the ERISA legislation and its liability standard for fiduciary investments (Williams 1978). Since smaller firms are clearly riskier investments, the impact of ERISA may be to reduce the supply of venture capital coming from financial institutions whose fiduciary managers must live within the constraint imposed by ERISA. State usury laws serve the same effect (Archer 1976, p. 59). While they may be designed to protect the unwise borrower from his taste for current consumption, they make it difficult for high risk firms to acquire debt funding at interest rates commensurate with their actual riskiness. Finally, investment tax credits can serve to place small firms at a relative net revenue disadvantage compared to large enterprise. As suggested above, small firms tend to be less capital intensive. Hence, investment credits on capital rather than labor investment could reduce production costs relatively less for smaller enterprises. These credits have the socially desirable purpose of spurring capital formation; thus, their potentially adverse impact on small enterprise is an inadvertent, but no less real, limit to new growth. They serve to give larger firms an artificial cost advantage that hurts the growth potential of smaller rivals.

The Impact of Competition Policy on Small Enterprise

The avowed purpose of the antitrust policies of the United States is to promote competition in the marketplace. Unfortunately, there can be great differences between purpose and performance. The administration of the antitrust laws provides several examples which suggest that the impact of the laws is either to protect the larger, established firms from the competition of smaller potential rivals or to force small firms to grow by merger (Brozen 1975). Such an outcome may be the result of strategic behavior on the part of larger, established firms (see chapter 6) or simply the inadvertent by-product of the antitrust law of enforcement procedures. In either case, antitrust policy may impose hidden burdens on small business which may be logically deduced, if not measured directly.

The efficiency of ownership integration, either horizontal, vertical, or conglomerate is one reason why large businesses become large. The essence of integration is the suppression of the price mechanism for certain transactions which would otherwise not be possible due to transaction failures (Williamson 1979; Klein et al. 1978). In each case the integrated firm is able to overcome some of the disadvantages associated with using the market mechanism to coordinate production or enjoy the various technological advantages integration conveys.

Firms may employ two separate strategies to effect an integrated structure. Integration may occur through internal growth or through purchasing companies that would fill gaps in the horizontal or vertical production chain. It may also occur through the establishment of contractual arrangements with other independent firms also in the horizontal or vertical production chain. These strategies may be referred to as ownership and contractual integration, respectively. Both tend to serve the same purpose of increasing the productive or distributive efficiency of the integrated enterprise relative to its nonintegrated competition. In the case of ownership integration, firms become large through merger; in the case of contractual integration, firms can grow because of increased efficiency yet still maintain their independent status. Examples of contractual integration include intrabrand territorial market division, resale price maintenance agreements, and long-term requirements contracts, among others.

Suppose a manufacturer produces a product which requires extensive local sales effort for maximum product quality at the retail level. Also suppose that for various reasons the manufacturer cannot use ownership integration to control the behavior of his retailers or distributors. This control is important because a failure on the part of this latter group to devote optimal resources to local sales effort diminishes product quality in the eyes of consumers and hurts the profits of the manufacturer (as well as those consumers who are quite willing to pay for high quality). Of course, retailers or distributors would gladly provide the optimal local sales effort if they could capture the rewards of this effort and cover their (higher) costs. But often they cannot do this, short of integration, due to a quirk in the private market mechanism (Bork 1978).

If there are several retailers or distributors in a given geographical area, each has an incentive to shirk in the provision of optimal local sales effort. Each knows that if he spends money on carrying a full line of products or hiring knowledgeable sales people, his costs will be higher than if he did not. No self-interested retailer will incur these costs if he believes that some other retailer or distributor of the same product will cut corners, lower prices (to reflect lower costs), and take away customers from the high-effort retailer. (After all, once a shopper has looked at the full line or talked with the informed sales people, he will still want to shop for price and buy at the low-priced competitor.) Thus, retailers and distributors will not engage in the optimal amount of local sales effort.

One way out of this is to have the manufacturing unit buy up retailers and/or distributors. But this solution is often impractical (a beer company would be hard pressed to buy up all the local retail outlets for its products, for example). An alternative is simply to divide up a given geographic region into exclusive sales territories and offer resale price maintenance agreements to would-be distributors. These allow the seller to capture the gains from providing optimal local sales effort since other distributors of the same brand are excluded from selling in the same territory (of course, this has no effect on competition since sellers of other brands can still do as they please). Maintaining retail prices by contract also serves the same purpose since they preclude *intrabrand* price cutting aimed at stealing customers away from rival retailers. Once again, there is no adverse impact on competition since the prices of other brands of the product are not affected. Unfortunately, these types of innovative responses to the local sales effort dilemma violate the letter of the antitrust laws. Hence, they preclude the use of contract integration by smaller firms that do not wish to integrate through conventional means. To the extent that the advantages of contract integration are not allowed smaller firms, their normal growth in market-share will be retarded. Though the antitrust laws seek to prevent anticompetitive practices, improper or unsophisticated enforcement may have a hidden adverse impact on small business.

Other contractual integrations such as certain exclusive dealing arrangements, vertical market divisions, long-term requirements contracts, and so forth are similarly proscribed by the antitrust authorities, with a similar negative impact on smaller, nonintegrated firms. Of course, if small nonintegrated firms cannot employ contracts to attain the efficiency necessary to compete with large firms, then it is predictable that organizational integrations, that is, mergers will be relied upon. The decision to merge or remain contractually integrated is a normal business decision. In the absence of government hostility to contractual integration, the relative costs and benefits of each form of integration would determine the matter. However, given the hostility to such contracts evidenced by the courts, the advantages of merger may often predominate. While this may not be viewed as a limit to growth, these policies may serve to inhibit the *internal* growth of small firms to the extent that such firms simply disappear through merger before they can grow by natural resource accumulation and market expansion.

Another artificial limit to growth may be embedded in the enforcement of the Robinson-Patman Anti-Chain Store Price Discrimination Act of 1936. This legislation was enacted ostensibly to protect small business from the predatory pricing practices of larger rivals. But, as sometimes occurs, legislative intent, administrative practice, and economic reality may diverge, producing ironic results. Some have argued that there is reason to suspect that the Robinson-Patman Act may be used now to preserve the market position of established larger firms against the aggressive competition of new and smaller competitors (Stone 1977; Bowman 1968). Local price cutting may be the only way for a new firm, small or otherwise, to establish itself in a market. New firms may treat sales below out-of-pocket costs as an investment in future market-share. Low prices, in a sense, substitute for advertising outlays. Banning the use of local price cutting, if not done carefully, may place new firms at a severe disadvantage to the already established firms in a market. If the established firms are also large while the newer firms are small, the implications for the development of small enterprise is straightforward. It is plausible that the Robinson-Patman Act has placed an excess burden on small enterprise, but is has not been verified empirically. Given the fact that predatory price cutting may be a viable dynamic strategy for incumbent firms, the net impact of the Robinson-Patman Act will have to remain unknown until such research is forthcoming.

Finally, it may be the case that market competition itself can have an adverse impact on the smaller firms in a given market. If so, competition policy that succeeds in intensifying the competitiveness of markets may serve as an inadvertent limit to growth of small firms. Owen has suggested that the businessman's dislike of "excessive" competition may make considerable economic sense. In his study of the welfare of small enterprises under differing competition pressure he found support for the hypothesis that stringent competition may reduce rates-of-return and growth potential of small firms. "Competition, if carried to an intense degree, would tend to retard, rather than accelerate, the emergence of large and more efficient units, reinforcing the vicious circle of smallness from which the small firm usually escapes only through extinction" (1971, p. 144). Thus, it may be the case that an overzealous antitrust policy (especially one based upon the number of firms in an industry as an indication of competition) could act as a regulatory limit to new growth. This hypothesis has been subjected to empirical verification with results which should give pause to antitrust enforcers (Owen 1971).

Patents: Help or Hinder to Firm Growth?

In the nineteenth century, there was considerable debate about the desirability of the patent system. Political economists typically characterized the patent debate in terms of free trade versus protectionism. The "free traders" lost in the legislatures but not without a strong battle.

Academic debate about patents paralleled public policy concerns. Economists' opinions were divided about the desirability of the patent system (Machlup and Penrose 1950). Reviewing earlier debates, Arnold Plant noted that J.B. Clark, like Bentham, believed that innovations would nearly cease without patents (1934). F.W. Taussig and A.C. Pigou took the opposite view that patents made little difference. Plant, also opposed to patents, noted the lack of rigor in most arguments on both sides. He criticized the common arguments made to support patents and offered arguments to the contrary. Although the economic impact of patents has been given consideration since Plant's 1934 article, there have been relatively few improvements in the quality of the arguments on either side (except for Kitch 1977).

Briefly, the case for patents has been that they are necessary to insure sufficient returns to innovative activities so that there is optimal investment in research and development. On the other side, it has been argued that patents are an imperfect system of reward that foster monopolies and over-reward some innovators.

A patent grants the holder a monopoly over the use of the patented invention for a specified time period. Although economists generally are opposed to monopoly, there seems to be general consensus that the patent system is desirable. The rationale for the patent system is that without ownership rights in inventions there would not be optimal allocation of resources to inventive activities, just as with any other valuable resource over which there are not well-defined legal rights. Just as a woodcutter would have less incentive to cut wood if bystanders were free to carry it away as fast as he cut it, inventors would have less incentive to produce inventions if anyone were free to use their ideas as soon as they were produced. Patents help establish the inventor's right to his invention in the same way that any other property right establishes ownership and marketable claims.

Using the patent system to produce legal rights over inventions has drawbacks. Rights to the use of an invention can be owned only by one party. Therefore, if independent parties are working simultaneously toward an invention, the first to produce the invention will receive a monopoly over its use, even though others may have been only a month behind. In some cases this will encourage inventors to work too intensively toward a patent so that their efforts will not be nullified by a competitor's patent. This system may produce a monopoly in a market characterized by competition before the patent issued. In addition, competitors have an incentive to develop substitute processes to avoid infringement of the patent when use of the patented process would be more economical. A substitute for patents which provides ownership rights to an invention without the governmental grant of a monopoly is the trade secret.

The U.S. Constitution gives Congress the power to grant patents. The first patent statute was passed in the early years of the Republic. The statutes have been amended numerous times since the 1790s and interpretations by the courts have been important in determining the effect of the law. If the holder of a patent believes his patent has ben infringed on by another, he may seek to enforce it by suit in federal court. The majority of patents reviewed in such cases are stricken as invalid. Many courts, including the Supreme Court, seem to believe that the Patent Office is too lenient in the application of the patent criteria.

Unlike patent law, the law of trade secrets arises from the common law. It provides "a common law property right in an invention that the courts will protect" (Seidel 1975). The availability of this protection for nonpatentable material and for patentable material that has been maintained confidential was emphasized by Chief Justice Burger in *Kewanee Oil Co.* v. *Bicron Corp.,* 416

U.S. 470 (1974), a case some thought would have meant the death of trade secrets had the decision gone the other way.

The primary common law basis for trade secrets is contract law. Individuals are free to contract for whatever secrecy they want and be held liable for breaches of secrecy so long as the contract is legal. Hence, one is protected by enforcement of contracts and by tort law, as stated in *4, Restatement, Torts* (1938):

> Par. 757. Liability for Disclosure of Use of Another's Trade Secret, General Principle
> One who discloses or uses another's trade secret, without a privilege to do so, is liable to the other if
> (a) he discovered the secret by improper means, or
> (b) his disclosure or use constitutes a breach of confidence respond in him by the other in disclosing the other if
> (c) he learned the secret from a third person with notice of the facts that it was a secret and that the third person discovered it by improper means or that the third person's disclosure of it was otherwise a breach of his duty to the other, or
> (d) he learned the secret with notice of the fact that it was a secret that its disclosure was made to him by mistake

Paragraph 758 states that an innocent discovery of a secret from a third person without notice that it is a secret relieves liability for a disclosure or use of the secret prior to notice of the fact of secrecy. Comment B to Paragraph 757 displays the greater breadth of coverage provided by secrecy law than is available under the patent law:

> A trade secret may consist of any formula, pattern device or complication of information which is used in one's business, and which give him an opportunity to obtain an advantage over competitors who do not know or use it. It may be a formula for a chemical compound, a process of manufacturing, treating or preserving materials, a pattern for a machine or other device, or a list of customers.

The subject matter must be secret but need not meet the standards of subject matter for patentable material. No civil authority decides whether or not the material qualifies. Coverage has included, among other things, news releases, plans for doing a radio program, methods of doing business (particular forms were involved), customer lists, credit ratings, blueprints, tables of data, and chemical processes. Once a trade secret loses secrecy, it is in the public domain. Violations of secrets may be punished by fines approximating the value of the loss suffered by the secret owner due to the theft and by an injunction against use of secrets by the thief for a certain time period.

Although it is true that in many instances trade secrecy provides less protection than does the ownership of a patent, that does not necessarily mean that patents are per se preferable. We do not know how the law of secrecy might have developed if patent law had never existed. Entrepreneurial incentives lead to new institutional arrangements under different legal constraints. If patents never existed, it is certain that secrecy laws would have been more important and developed further and that entrepreneurs would have adopted various techniques to protect and prosper from innovations. Hirschleifer (1971) has explained some institutional arrangements in nonpatent situations.

He argues that there are returns that could be earned by innovators above and beyond the return for the use of the innovation. The innovator has access to information about his innovation before others in the market and can make investments based upon this information which might be far more valuable than the royalties from patents and copyrights. Hirschleifer gives as an example Eli Whitney's invention of the cotton gin. Armed with information about a superior method for processing cotton, Whitney could have invested in cotton and cotton-bearing land, in businesses engaging in the selling-warehousing and transporting of cotton, and in a number of other speculative activities concerning both cotton, substitutes for cotton (for example wool), and complementary goods (textiles, machinery). As Hirschleifer notes, the innovator possesses valuable information concerning the investment prospects of both complements and substitutes for his invention. The use of this investment information may be all the incentive that an innovator needs to produce the optimal amount of innovation, and the granting of monopoly rights to the innovator may entail net social costs rather than benefits.

There are individual and industrial success stories in which patents were not important. It is useful to consider these instances, because they help us to understand better how a world without patents could operate. In certain cases, such as Coca-Cola and Smith's Brothers cough drops, trade secrecy has provided decades of protection far superior to the limited returns which would have occurred under patent law. At the time of invention, seventeen years of protection may appear lengthy to the inventor, but, in the case of Coca-Cola, the returns under a patent would have been a minute fraction of the returns generated by secrecy. Other industries, such as the customer list industry, rely on law of secrecy for protection. Casual observation of the growth of that industry in recent years would seem to confirm the possibility of prosperity in the absence of patent protection. Whether or not the growth would have been greater with patents (or copyright) is, of course, unknown.

It is impossible to discuss the operation of patent law without considering antitrust law. The compatibility or the conflict of these laws has been a subject of controversy. Bowman asserts that the laws are not in conflict and that both "have a common central economic goal: *to maximize wealth by producing what consumers want at the lowest cost*" (1973), p. 1).

Contrary to this position, the economics literature on bureaucracy suggests that federal agencies do not, by the nature of the bureaucratic process, maximize the well being of consumers (Niskanen 1971; Tullock 1965). Perhaps without patent law and without antitrust law, the market would be better able to serve consumers. The coexistence of patent and antitrust law is an example of the second-best nature of economic organization directed by a central authority. The powers given by patent law appeared to be so strong that, rather than limit that law, it was limited in effect by another set of constraints, the antitrust law.

Antitrust statutes were designed to do more than limit the monopolistic powers granted by patents, but the combination has led to the repression of numerous contractual forms of organizations which would have arisen in the absence of such constraints. If patent powers never existed, then fewer restraints on contractual organizations would have been believed necessary by the legislature and the courts. Under these conditions, the law of secrecy, combined with the law of contract, would have fostered the development of various institutional arrangements to guarantee profits for successful inventors. The following cases provide examples of institutions that might exist without patent and antitrust laws.

In a well-known antitrust case, *Fashion Orginators' Guild of America* v. *Federal Trade Commission*, 312 U.S. 457 (1941), the Supreme Court affirmed a decree of the Federal Trade Commission (FTC) ordering the Fashion Originators' Guild of America (Guild) "to cease and desist from certain practices found to have been done in combination and to constitute 'unfair methods of competition' tending to monopoly." Mr. Justice Black explained the facts:

> The garment manufacturers claim to be creators or original and distinctive designs of fashionable clothes for women, and the textile manufacturers claim to be creators of similar original fabric designs. After these designs enter the channels of trade, other manufacturers systematically make and sell copies of them, the copies usually selling at prices lower than the garments copied. Petitioners call this practice of copying unethical and immoral, and give it the name of "style piracy." And although they admit that their "original creations" are neither copyrighted nor patented, and indeed assert that existing legislation affords them no protection against copyists, they nevertheless urge that sale of copied designs constitutes an unfair trade practice and a tortious invasion of their rights. Because of these alleged wrongs, petitioners, while continuing to compete with one another in many respects, combined among themselves to combat and, if possible, destroy all competition from the sale of garments which are copies of their "original creations." They admit that to destroy such competition

they have in combination purposely boycotted and declined to sell their products to retailers who follow a policy of selling garments copied by other manufacturers from designs put by Guild members.

About twelve thousand retailers nationwide signed agreements with the Guild not to carry copies of registered designs. In 1936, the 176 manufacturers of women's garments that belonged to the Guild sold over 38 percent of all women's garments wholesaling for $6.75 or more, and over 60 percent of those at $10.75 and above. Similarly, some producers of textiles agreed to sell their products only to those manufacturers who belonged to the Guild.

The Guild maintained a Design Registration Bureau for garments, and a similar organization was established for textiles. Employees of the Guild visited retail stores to see if the agreement was being violated by either cooperating retailers, who might sell copies of registered designs, or by manufacturers, who might be selling to noncooperating retailers. Following a detailed procedure for trial and appeal within the Guild, a retailer or manufacturer who violated the contract would be fined. Obviously, in a competitive market, without enforcement the Guild would have been ineffective.

In addition to protecting members from the copying of original designs, the Guild undertook other activities, including imposing advertising restrictions on its members, regulating some of the contract terms that members could offer customers, regulating days on which special sales could be held, and restricting members from doing business with certain firms. The Court decided against the Guild by finding that it violated the Sherman Act by restricting competition in the women's garment industry.

The Court's interpretation of antitrust law is not an issue here. Rather, the following analysis suggests that the Fashion Originator's Guild case demonstrates the ability of the market to produce an alternative to a governmental system of patents. Under some circumstances, the market system of protection for innovators may be superior to the governmentally operated system.

The Guild did provide some monopoly power for its members. The Guild must have produced benefits for members to have been willing to join. However, it did not have complete monopoly power over the industry. There was no governmental protection for the Guild, and there was free entry into both dress manufacturing and retailing. Indeed, a substantial proportion of both manufacturers and retailers remained out of the Guild. The Guild is an example of the private contracts that would arise to protect innovations were no patent protection available. Because of the Guild's agreements not to copy the original designs of other Guild members, members were afforded some degree of protection for their investments in innovative activity. The original designs also had an exclusive outlet in the retail market, allowing for market segmentation.

Another example of contractual protection for a product that is difficult to protect concerns the Associated Press (AP). Prior to *Associated Press* v. *United States* 321 U.S. 1 (1945), when the Supreme Court struck down the arrangement, there was a contract among news gathers and disseminators to protect news. The practice has been allowed by *International News Service* v. *Associated Press,* 248 U.S. 215 (1918), which effectively recognized the existence of property rights in news.

A cooperative association of newspapers controlled the use of news gathered by member newspapers, employees of the Associated Press, and cooperating foreign news service. Members agreed to sell their news only to the AP, for use by paying members. By this arrangement, enforced by fines and suspensions from the Association, news services agreed to provide their news exclusively to Association members in return for the exclusive use of news produced by other Association members. There were costly entry restrictions to reduce the number of entrants that would compete with existing members.

The court struck down the Association as a violation of the antitrust laws. The primary result was that newspapers then had to purchase copyrighted news, that is, news given protection by the government, rather than news protected by voluntary contract. As in the case of the Fashion Originators' Guild, there was no protection from competing associations, or was protection by governmental copyright essential, although common law specification of property rights could provide similar protection.

If patent (or copyright) protection were not afforded innovators for their innovations, they would have an incentive to try to secure rights to the innovations through private contracts. Firms could form a guild that (in the same manner as the Fashion Originators' Guild) would make exclusive retailing agreements with retailers while agreeing among themselves not to copy each other's innovations. Retailers who sold any product not produced by guild members would not be able to stock any products of guild members.

The guild members would have an incentive to enter into this arrangement for two reasons. First, it affords the members protection from some potential copying of their innovations. Second, the guild may be able to exercise some monopoly power in the market to increase the profits of members. To the extent that the guild exercises monopoly power, individual firms would have an incentive to cheat or to drop out of the guild in order to capture a greater share of the market.

Retailers have an incentive to enter into an agreement with the guild in order to carry products that contain the latest innovations. Although nonmembers may copy the innovations of guild members, the innovator is able to market first so that imitators may copy the innovation only after they have seen it. Therefore, retailers could not be assured of having the most advanced products to sell unless they purchased from guild members.

Such contracts are not seen in most markets because innovations are protected by patent and because a guild like the one described would be in violation of the Sherman Act. In the absence of these two factors, such arrangements could be envisioned in any industry which produced valuable innovations.

Given the contractual alternative to government protection of the rights to innovations, questions arise about the consequences of each system. The first question is whether the patent system enhances production possibilities over the contract system. This is related to the issue of whether the patent system causes an overinvestment in innovative activity. If it does, then the contract system, which in many industries would provide fewer incentives to innovate, might be superior unless it leads to underinvestment in innovation because of insufficient protection of new developments. Here the assumption is that the technological advances produced under a patent system will enable the economy to be technologically more productive than would the contract alternative. The disadvantage of the patent system is the increased monopoly power that the innovator has over the use of his innovation compared to most contractual arrangements.

When comparing the social costs and benefits of a patent system with a system of trade secrets, the calculus hinges upon whether the cost of increased monopoly power in the case of patents outweighs the benefits from increased innovation that may result from patents. The increased monopoly cost is clear since the government guarantees a monopoly. If patents increase innovative activity, then they will provide the more desirable system only if the value of the increased innovation exceeds the welfare loss resulting from additional monopoly power.

In the case if the Fashion Originators' Guild the amount of monopoly power wielded by the Guild was probably quite small. A substantial portion of the industry was not under the control of the Guild, and there was free entry into all phases of the women's garment industry. Under the Guild arrangement, therefore, the losses due to monopoly were small, yet there were incentives to invest in some design innovation. There is no reason to suspect that patents would produce optimal results in the women's garment industry or, perhaps, in any other industry.

Other factors enter into the consideration of alternative institutional arrangements to protect the rights to innovations. If guilds were allowed for this purpose, they might be able to restrain trade in other ways, thus, creating another set of monopoly problems. This issue would revolve around the ability of government decision makers to enforce rules against collusion for purposes other than protection of innovations. This may not be a problem since there are many trade associations and professional groups that meet for legal purposes but are prevented from certain illegal practices.

Under the patent system, on the other hand, the government enforces the monopoly right of an innovator to the use of the innovation. The same incentives for collusion to maximize joint profits exist in either case, but there is government sanction of some monoply rights in one case. These factors suggest that innovation-protecting guilds operating in a world of voluntary contracts would not be able to apply a substantial amount of monoply power to the markets in which they operate. This argument is made under the assumption that guilds would not be sanctioned by the government, except in the judicial enforcement of legitimate contracts. Guilds would try to receive government protection for monopolistic activities beyond that available by contract. As long as this potential for abuse is avoided, guilds would seem justifiable.

Although there has been no mention of trade secret law in the discussion of the guilds, its importance is obvious as part of contract law. In the Fashion Originators Guild, although there was no trade secret issue, trade secrecy was used. Designers kept their innovations secret until they were ready to market them. This secrecy gives innovators an extra time advantage over imitators, who will be later in marketing the goods than the innovators. Because of this time advantage, innovators can exploit their creations at what they perceive to be the optimal price, knowing that imitations will be appearing within a certain time. This allows less monopoly exploitation of the consumer than the seventeen years provided by patents.

It is difficult to imagine what organizational forms would have emerged in the market and what differences there would be in the present laws of trade secrecy if patent law had not existed. Even though the present laws of trade secrecy are probably not as well developed and sophisticated as they would be if patents were not so widely available, the law does appear to provide sufficient protection to innovators in some instances. Our purpose is not to advocate the replacement of the patent system, but to illustrate that viable market alternatives might have emerged were they allowed to do so. Based on the few examples reviewed here, it may be argued that patents have served to make it more difficult for smaller firms to compete with larger established firms.

Securities Regulation

Federal securities regulation emerges from the Securities Act of 1933 and the Securities Exchange Act of 1934. The earlier law was designed to regulate initial offerings of securities; the later act regulates the trading of securities previously issued. The thrust of the 1933 Act is the requirement that no person may sell a security unless a registration statement if filed with the Securities Exchange Commission. The effects of filing costs and restrictions on firm development will be discussed in this section. The 1934 Act requires that corporations of a certain size file a variety of periodic reports with the SEC; this law is of interest to small businesses if their stock is publically traded or when they grow to have five hundred stockholders and $1 million of assets.

Of particular interest to small enterprises are the series 140 rules promulgated by the SEC which restrict the issuance of securities by firms seeking to raise capital for expansion. James C. Sargent, a former SEC Commissioner, has concluded that "often reviewing these statutes with an eye toward small business, it becomes increasingly obvious that, literally, there is no way that small business can live in the framework of these statutory and regulatory provisions" (1978, p. 903). An examination of these regulations reveals that in addition to the dollar costs of compliance, they serve to attenuate the utility of the corporate form of organization for small firms.

As an example, consider the impact of SEC Rule 144. This regulation requires that an investor assuming an equity position in a new venture must wait two years to get his money out of the company if, for some reason, he wishes to sell his shares. If a person acquires securities in a nonpublic transaction and holds them for two years, he can sell whichever is less: 1 percent of the total outstanding shares; or the average weekly reported volume of trading over the four weeks prior to the filing of a Form 144 notice of sales that is required of listed companies. For unlisted companies, an investor can sell no more than 1 percent of the total outstanding shares of the original issuing company in any six month period. The impact of Rule 144 on the willingness of investors to take equity positions in such illiquid new ventures is obvious.

Sargent has noted that the 140 series of Rules has discouraged many large investors from supporting new, innovative small businesses. For example, if an investor placed a million dollars in a new company, . . . "that investor would have to wait two years before he can get his money out, and then, he can only get out to the extent of one percent of the total equity interest outstanding. It would therefore take him two or three lifetimes to recap his investment (1978, p. 903). The real impact of these securities regulations has been to remove from small firms one of the primary attributes of the corporate form of organization—easy alienability of ownership. Many advantages of the corporate form of organization are, in large part, denied small ventures.

Several definitions of the private business corporations have been offered; most emphasize the contractual nature of their organizational form and the fact that ownership is several and, especially, easily terminated.

Jensen and Meckling (1976, p. 311) define the corporation as "simply one form of legal fiction which serves as an excess for contracting relationships and which is also characterized by the existence of divisible residual claims on the assets and cash flows of the organization which can generally be sold *without permission of the other contracting individuals.*" Henry Manne writes that "one of the greatest advantages of large corporate system is that it allows individuals to use small fractions of these savings for various purposes, without risking a disastrous loss of any corporation in which they have invested becomes insolvent . . . (1967, p. 263). For most investors liquidity for marketability of securities is their most important attribute. Investments may be transacted at low cost at almost any time.

Rule 144 does not suggest a near permanent investment; it requires it as a matter of federal law. Since the evolution of the corporate form may be explained, in large part, as a least-cost method of organizing production, Rule 144 serves to raise an explicit cost barrier to the expansion of small business via the issuance of new equities. Whatever the other attractions of investing in small ventures, the inability to easily alienate ownership interest will restrict capital formation in small enterprise. Thus, as Sargent (1978, p. 904) notes, "It seems obvious that the current statutory and regulatory guidelines must be changed if they are to help small business entrepreneurial investors and get them to come back and to support enterprising fledgling small business companies."

Despite the importance of state and federal securities regulations with respect to capital markets, relatively few studies have measured the impact of the rules regarding the reporting of financial information (disclosure requirements). Professor Benston noted that before the 1964 articles by Professors Stigler and Friend, there had been no examination of the economic rationale for the regulation of the securities markets (1973). While the studies that will be reviewed here provide important insights into the issues regarding impact of the federal securities laws, it will be obvious that the studies generally do not address the impact of state securities law, the impact of federal securities laws on small business, or the impact of the laws with respect to the life cycle of firms.

Stigler examined the impact of federal securities regulations on stock performance by comparing stock performance in the 1920s, before regulation, to performance in the 1950s, when the 1933 and 1934 laws were operational in a nonwar and nondepression economy. Stigler concluded that "SEC registration requirements had no important effect on the quality of new securities sold to the public" (1964, p. 124).

Of particular interest to small business is Stigler's finding, after examining stock issues in the 1920s of between $500 thousand and $1 million compared to larger stock offerings, that "there was no systematic or statistically significant variation of price with size of issue (1964, p. 120). Other parts of

Stigler's study concerned price fixing by members of the NYSE for broker services and other market controls that are not relevant here.

Friend and Herman, one a former SEC official, immediately came to rescue the SEC by charging that Stigler's study was completely lacking in merit (1964). Most of the issues they discuss have little relevance to this study, and others have since been resolved in a more sophisticated manner. Friend and Herman find all SEC activities discussed to be beneficial and, reviewing Stigler's data, conclude the opposite: That SEC registration requirements did improve stock performance for all stocks, large and small offerings. Robbins and Werner, former and current SEC employees, responded at the same time that Stigler was incorrect (1964). They failed, however, to present any empirical refutation of Stigler's study.

Stigler responded to the two sets of critics, first by castigating their methodological approach to the topic, then by reexplaining his tests. Responding to Friend and Herman, after reviewing their tests and his, Stigler concludes again the SEC review procedure did not significantly improve the market performance of new issues relative to outstanding issues (1964 "Comment", p. 419). Friend and Herman responded to Stigler by reiterating their earlier statistical evidence that SEC disclosure requirements had improved stock performance (1965).

More detailed investigations of the impact of certain securities laws and studies indicating the structure of the capital market to help form securities policies did not emerge until the 1970's. Brown performed an empirical test to determine the relative success/failure rates of new issue stocks under different market conditions (1970). In its 1963 *Report of the Special Study of the Securities Markets* the SEC concluded, on the basis of sketchy evidence, that it was not surprised "that lack of success should be so common among new, small ventures brought to the public during a period of high market receptivity" (Brown 1979, p. 10). No policy recommendations were made on this basis alone. Using accepted market measurement devices, Brown looked at the success/failure rates of initial stock offerings by new firms entering the securities market during receptive and unreceptive times from the late 1940s through the mid-1950s. He found that the failure rate was significantly higher for new firm issues during unreceptive markets than for the sample of new firm issues during receptive market periods. Since there is no a priori reason to expect that the business success rates of the firms in the sample should be different, Brown hypothesized that the result was simply caused by general investor opinion at particular points in time and because the SEC tends to retard new issues during receptive market time periods. Even though costs are higher during receptive periods, due to overall better stock market conditions, investors are more receptive to new issues during those times, so the SEC should take no position about the desirability of new issues during different times according to stock market conditions.

Probably the most famous study of the impact of securities laws on the stock market is Benston's 1973 article about the 1934 Securities Exchange Act. He reviewed the usefulness of disclosure requirements of the SEC for stocks falling under such requirements. Like some previous studies, which are summarized by Benston, he found that the disclosure rules have not increased the accuracy of information provided to investors. Some SEC accounting practices encourage the production of numbers that are not meaningful, although other conventions are useful, so that in net there may be no improvement (1973, p. 135). Further, like other studies, Benston found that the financial statement data were accurate but did not predict future economic conditions or were completely discounted by the market before they were published, so that the data were not useful to investors by the time the SEC required disclosure. Empirical support for the efficient market hypothesis further displays that since there is no difference in the rate-of-return earned by professional investment analysts than what would be earned by any diversified market portfolio, the data required by SEC disclosure is no more useful to professional investors than it is to members of the public.

Next, Benston estimated whether the market performed better after the SEC disclosure requirements were implemented than it did before the rules existed. He tested five hypotheses:

1. To hide poor performance managers avoid disclosure.
2. Not realizing the value of information to investors, managers failed to disclose.
3. The costs imposed on corporations by required disclosure are greater than the benefits to stockholders.
4. "Required disclosure results in benefits to the market as a whole because investors would prefer stocks on registered exchanges to alternative investments. . . . However, some costs are imposed on those firms that would not otherwise have disclosed.
5. Required disclosure did not impose sufficient costs or benefits to be measured" (Benston 1973, p. 144).

Empirical tests only supported the fifth hypothesis, that the disclosure provisions were of no apparent value to investors.

Further, Benston tested whether companies that did not disclose income prior to the imposition of the rules offered a different rate-of-return than companies that voluntarily disclosed. He found that the nondisclosure firms outperformed the firms that did disclose. He guessed that the reason for the difference was that the firms that disclosed were known to be riskier, so that they had to be more open with financial information to attract and reassure investors. Benston also determined that the 1934 Act did not reduce the riskiness of securities. Stocks before and after the Act conformed to a random walk and there was no change in overall performance after the rules were implemented.

In sum, Benston concluded "that the disclosure requirements of the Securities Exchange Act of 1934 had no measurable positive effect on the securities traded on the NYSE. There appears to have been little basis for the legislation and no evidence that it was needed or desirable. Certainly there is doubt that more required disclosure is warranted" (1973, p. 153).

As in the case of the Stigler article in 1964, Irwin Friend came to the defense of the SEC. He asserted that Benston's tests failed to show what he asserted they showed: " . . . Benston's regressions considerably understate the usefulness of published financial statements" (Friend and Westerfield 1975, p. 468). Benston's evidence was characterized as "weak" and not supportive of the conclusion "that the 1934 Act had no effect on stock market prices" (1975, p. 470). Further, Friend and Westerfield claimed that none of Benston's tests are " . . . relevant to the fairness of the market as between corporate or market insiders and public investors" (1975, p. 471).

Since Friend and Westerfield failed to present any alternative empirical tests to Benston's, it is difficult to evaluate the arguments. Benston replied to Friend and Westerfield point to point, reiterating his arguments of the original paper. He concluded that the reader would "find evidence and additional substantive empirical tests upon which the conclusion of my paper is based" by reading the paper in light of the criticisms (1975, p. 476).

Friend and Blume (1975, p. 916) did reply, indirectly, to some of Benston's arguments in an article published later that year. There they showed that the standard deviation of the rate of return on New York Stock Exchange stocks as a whole was smaller in the decades 1942-1951, 1952-1961, and 1962-1971 (post-SEC) than for the decades 1922-1931 (pre-SEC) and 1932-1941 (part-SEC).

In 1970 many firms reported for the first time in their 10-K reports revenues and profits by product lines. This change in disclosure rules by the SEC allowed for an interesting test of the usefulness of information not available to the public previously. Since 1970, firms with more than one line-of-business have to report sales and profits before taxes and extraordinary items by product-line. In 1970, firms were required to provide this information back to 1966. Previously, most firms only made public their financial information on a consolidated basis. Collins tested the usefulness of this information (1975).

Collins determined, from empirical tests of market performance before and after the information became available, that "provided that the costs of disclosing such information are minimal, this finding would suggest that the SEC's product-line disclosures are warranted because they provide information useful to investors in assessing future earnings changes" (1975, p. 132). Further, Collins found that "while disclosure of sales by segments may be useful to investors, disclosure of profit figures is not" (1975, p. 146).

In sum, Collins estimated that the use of segment revenue data allowed investors to predict future stock performance. While there were fewer unexpected results because of the better data, there were no differences in the average return, which indicates that the market was efficient with respect to the nonpublic segment data (1975, p. 156). This finding of the impact of the 1970 requirements seems consistent with the general findings of most studies on SEC disclosure requirements: The rate-of-return is not changed because of better information, but there is less variance in returns so that overall risk has been reduced.

Horowitz and Kolodny did a study similar to that by Collins of the effect of the SEC's line-of-business reporting requirements. Their study was more comprehensive than that of Collins because they chose two sets of fifty firms. One set was required to report for the first time on a line-of-business basis during 1971, and the other set was not required to do so. Data for the two sets were collected for a nine-year time period. "The null hypothesis that the required disclosure had no effect on the risk and return of securities close to the time of its reporting could not be rejected at the 0.05 level in any of the tests. Thus, the authors' results provide no evidence in support of the universally accepted contention that the SEC required disclosure furnished investors with valuable information" (Horowitz and Kolodny 1977, p. 247). The authors concluded that, given the costs of reporting requirements, the SEC should be required to offer strong evidence of the need for such information before implementing rules which seem to have low benefits. This view probably summarizes the general evidence from academic studies of SEC required disclosure: There are benefits, but they appear to be small, so requirements should be used judiciously.

In 1976, Archer made the simple point that the cost of floating new securities declines as a percent of the size of the offering, the larger the offering (1976, p. 60). He cited SEC data showing that for stock issuances under $0.5 million, the costs of marketing the issue averaged 27 percent of the issue. The percent drops to one-tenth that level for very large stock offerings because many of the costs of marketing new issues are fixed. The disclosure requirements of the SEC have generally been the same regardless of size of offering, so the requirements serve as a regressive tax on small business offerings. Recent moves by the SEC to make Regulations A offerings more useful appear to be partly alleviating this problem.

Phillips and Zecher have estimated that, as of 1975, the cost to small companies (average assets of $26 million) of complying with SEC mandatory periodic disclosure rules equalled 0.0723 percent of their assets per year (1981, chap. 3). This is thirty-three times as costly as it is for large firms (average assets of $2.6 billion), for which the annual cost was 0.0022 percent of assets. Disclosure requirements will always have the effect of a regressive tax on businesses according to asset size, so long as the reporting requirements are essentially the same for all public firms regardless of size. This does not necessarily mean that the reporting requirements are not justified, only that they do serve as a small competitive detriment to small organizations using public equity markets.

Miscellaneous Inadvertent Impacts of Policy on Small Business

Several other inadvertent impacts of public or private policy upon the successful progress of small enterprises may be identified. These include the anticompetitive price effects of ICC truck regulation, the adverse impact of energy mismanagement on small firms which rely heavily upon transportation to serve their markets, the impacts of Financial Accounting Standards Board rules on small enterprise, and numerous others.

Adam Smith once observed that the economies of scale are limited by the extent of the market. Stated simply, firms may grow larger and enjoy the competitive technological and integrational advantages of large scale production as long as market demand will support production at large volumes. Of course, one of the factors limiting market demand is the ability to transport goods long distances from the point of manufacture. When competing with their larger rivals, small firms may suffer a comparative disadvantage when transportation costs, or the availabilities of transportation services, change. For example, when energy prices rise, or fuel becomes unavailable, it may be the case that smaller firms suffer more since larger firms may have established long-term supply relationships which protect them more from the adverse consequences of either of these phenomena.

Similarly, regulation of the transportation industry by the ICC may have a more adverse impact upon small enterprise (Brozen 1975, p. 10). Unlike small firms, larger manufacturers may have the size to justify a fleet of transport vehicles, which isolates them from the monopolistic prices associated with protectionist ICC regulation. Smaller firms usually cannot justify such fleets and must rely upon regulated contract carriers. These factors can impose an absolute cost disadvantage upon smaller firms. However, unlike other absolute cost differences, these result from specific public policies. The extent of their impact on small enterprise growth could be roughly estimated from an investigation of the relative importance of transportation as a factor of production for small and large firms. If it is true that smaller firms are relatively more "transportation intensive," then the adverse impacts of federal energy policy and transportation regulation may be ascertained. As with the other regulatory constraints on small business discussed in this section, the literature does not yield such tests as yet.

Finally, not all policies which have potential adverse impacts on small business are public. For example, it has been charged that despite other benefits to investors, the uniform reporting standards required by the Financial Accounting Standards Board serve as a regressive tax on small business (Armstrong 1977).

The need for authoritative accounting information is based, in part, on the nature of corporate organizations. As corporations grow, and increase capitalization from equity shares, the number of individual "owners" increases, sometimes dramatically. Some firms have millions of owners. As a result of this, there naturally occurs a need to separate the ownership function from the management of the firm. Delegated authority raises an accountability problem which can be solved, in part, by authoritative accounting and disclosure. However, it follows, from the nature of the problem, that the value of such a solution is in direct proportion to the size of the enterprise. For smaller firms the value of investor information is less since there is a smaller "distance" between ownership and control. Despite this, FASB rules have been applied uniformly to all firms, with no distinction on the basis of size and, hence, with marginal benefit from the information required. This can impose a regressive tax on small firms in several ways. First, it may very well be the case that there are certain fixed costs associated with the preparation of financial statements. To the extent that this is so, larger firms are better able to spread these costs over larger outputs. Second, larger firms may employ in-house staff that could be used in the preparation of financial statements during slack times; smaller firms may have to hire their accounting services in the marketplace. Third, uniform standards force all firms to provide the same information categories; some of this information is useless to the small firm while the large, multidivision firm would produce it for internal use anyway. The extent to which uniform FASB rules act as a regressive tax on small business has yet to be subjected to empirical investigation. However, it is clear that they may impose an artificial-regulatory limit on the growth of small firms.

In summary, this chapter has illustrated how a variety of public policies, manifested as regulations, may have an inadvertent chilling effect on the growth and potential development of new and smaller firms. While these policies may serve other legitimate purposes, their impact upon small firms cannot be ignored.

6

Artificial-Strategic Barriers to Firm Growth

It is always in the interest of established firms to limit the ability of their rivals, potential and existing, to compete for the same business. When such limitations take the form of efficient adaptations to market and production opportunities, the limits to new growth faced by the newer and smaller firms are virtually inevitable and not properly the subject of public intervention. However, when the dominant firms in an industry seek to limit the competitive activity of their rivals by patently inefficient short-run behavior, pursued in the hope that it will payoff over the long-run, public concern is merited.

Any activities inhibiting the growth of smaller firms which are not based upon economic efficiency will be referred to as artificial-strategic limits to growth. They are artificial in that they represent acts that would not be pursued by a wealth-maximizing firm in the absence of competitive pressure from potential or existing rivals; that is, they are inefficient per se. They are strategic in that they are pursued by the dominant firm(s) in an industry for the primary purpose of establishing, maintaining, or consolidating a monopolistic position in the market. Acts which are designed to increase the efficiency of operations may serve to eliminate less efficient and, perhaps, smaller rivals. But these acts will not be treated as artificial-strategic barriers to growth because the elimination of rivals need not have been the primary intent of the action and/or the elimination of inefficient rivals is socially productive.

In the industrial organization/antitrust literature, artificial-strategic barriers are given several titles. Among the most common are abusive trade practices, unfair competition, and artificial barriers to entry. The list of potential artificial-strategic limits to new growth is long. To organize the discussion, two types of artificial-strategic limits to new growth may be identified. First, there are the behaviors directed at specific existing industrial rivals. These activities which are referred to in the literature as abusive trade practices or unfair methods of competition include any type of predatory conduct on the part of established firms. The other broad category of artificial-strategic limits encompasses less focused attacks on potential or existing rivals and covers all conduct generally referred to in the literature as artificial barriers to entry. The two categories of strategic behavior will be discussed in turn.

Predation

The primary requisite for enjoying the benefits of monopoly is restricting output relative to the level associated with greater competition. Without some means of output restriction, prices will be bid down and will just cover the opportunity costs of production. Since small competitors wish to expand output in order to equate rising marginal costs with market prices, output restriction by a dominant firm in a competitive market is difficult, though necessary to maintain monopoly status. Since there is some gross correlation between the number of firms in a market and the ability to extract monopoly rents from consumers, part of the rational strategic behavior of a potential monopolist would include the elimination of actual and potential competitors from his market (Cournot 1960, chap. 7; Chamberlin 1948). It is obviously easier for output to be restricted when only one firm is supplying output, than when a number of rivals are ready to spoil such plans. The attractiveness of certain pricing practices and methods of unfair competition which have the intent of reducing competition by eliminating competitors is thus established. Several forms of such behavior have been discussed in the literature. Predatory pricing (including unjustified volume discounts), limit pricing, and conscious attempts to foreclose competitive opportunities through exclusionary practices provide key examples.

Economic predation goes by many names (for example, cutthroat competition, price discrimination, unfair competition, local price cutting, price wars, and so forth), but the idea is uniformly simple. In order to eliminate competition, a large and dominant firm in a market may try to drive out smaller and weaker competitors or induce them to merge with the dominant firm, or it may form a price-fixing conspiracy by charging selectively low prices in their markets. To be able to engage in such a practice, the dominant firm must have adequate resources to suffer the losses entailed by below-cost pricing for the period of time required to eliminate the competition. In other words, a small independent competitor must eventually bend to the will of the larger firm which can reach deeper into its "long purse" to finance an extended price war. To say the least, the rationality of such a business tactic for large dominant firms is a contested issue.

Opposition to the conventional wisdom of predatory pricing is widespread among economists and lawyers; it centers on the proposition that among all possible strategies available to large firms which may be employed to eliminate competition, this one has the lowest expected payoff (McGee 1958; Koller 1975; Telser 1965; Bork 1978, chap. 7). Outright mergers would make more business sense than price wars according to this line of criticism. Since the large firm selling below cost incurs greater absolute losses than small firms during the price war, the benefits, over time, associated with the strategy need to be great if this is to be a rational strategy. Yet the problem of reentry of the crushed firm's physical assets decreases the expected value of the entire operation: Unlike a real war, a price war results only in bankruptcy, not in the outright destruction of physical assets. Relatively certain short-run profits must be sacrificed for rather uncertain future profits, which to the cynics' basic conclusion: Evidence of a predatory pricing episode is more consistent with the notion that businessmen occasionally choose irrational strategies than with the notion that predatory pricing is a genuine threat to small competitors. As Telser notes, "Price warfare between the two (firms) is equivalent to forming a coalition between each firm and the consumers, such that the consumers gain from the conflict between the firms. Since both firms can benefit by agreeing on a merger price, one would think that rational men would prefer merger" (1966, p. 265).

This logical approach to the price war strategy is not convincing to a number of commentators who recognize that while the "kill the rival" theory is not compelling in a static environment, such an environment is not what real world firms face (Yamey 1972; Williamson 1977). In a dynamic context, the mere threat of a price war may affect the plans of new entrants or smaller existing firms, inducing them to sell out or stay out *in anticipation of* a price-cutting episode. As Yamey notes, "A bout of price warfare initiated by the aggressor, or a threat of such activity, might serve to cause the rival to revise its expectations, and hence to alter its terms of sale to an acceptable level" (1972, p. 130). Williamson (1977, p. 284) reemphasizes this crucial point: "Predatory pricing involves strategic behavior in which intertemporal considerations are central. Static economic models that fail to capture these attributes miss crucial features of the predatory pricing issue."

In other words, even if a price war is risky and uneconomic on a one-shot basis, the predatory firm may wish to invest in such a strategy as an advertisement to would be rivals that entry will be punished. The irrationality argument can be refuted easily if aggressive responses to entry in some markets can deter entry in other markets. "If by responding aggressively to current threat of entry a dominant firm can give a "signal" that it intends to react vigorously to entry in later time periods or different geographical regions, discounted future gains may more than offset sacrifices of current profit" (Williamson 1977, p. 287). Given the unsettled state of the debate, the question of whether or not local price cutting (and volume discounts) by larger firms represents a genuine barrier to new growth is unanswerable without further thought and empirical research. However, other forms of predation may be of immediate interest to small enterprises and public policy makers.

A potentially more important form of predation involves the misuse of governmental process as a competitive weapon. In general, the costs of litigating cases in the courts and before administration agencies tend to be similar for each business party involved. Included in a full reckoning of such costs are not only out-of-pocket expenses but also the diversion of-executive talent from productive activities. Litigation need not have merit for considerable expense to be generated; as a result, firms may use the legal process to impose costs on rivals. As Bork (1978, p. 159) observes, "Where the object of predatory litigation is to drive an existing rival from a market altogether, the technique will generally be useful only by a larger firm against a smaller, since equal absolute costs will be proportionately greater for the smaller firm."

In addition, economists have for some time argued that governmental processes can be used by private firms to advance their special interest without regard to, or in direct opposition to, the public interest (Stigler 1971). The economic theory of regulation posits that regulatory agencies eventually become captives of the industries they were formed to regulate. Some scholars have asserted that government process in general is often employed to foster the interests of established firms by blocking the advance of new, smaller rivals—the triumph of the status quo ante (Stone 1977). Some of the trade regulations administered by the Federal Trade Commission may have this adverse impact on small business, despite the fact that the FTC may in other cases be a protector of small enterprise (Narver and Preston 1976, p. 18; Posner 1973). For example, the enforcement of the FTC Act's restrictions on aggressive advertising practices may impose a tax on new enterprises which must use that method to penetrate the markets of established firms.

Since deception is illegal per se, and virtually all advertising deviates from the strict truth, established firms fearing the inroads of new aggressive rivals for their market-share may use the FTC as a barrier to entry (Posner 1973). Under current FTC procedures, the cost of litigating a deceptive practice case falls on the firm accused of the practice and the Commission, not on the firm filing the complaint. This gives established firms the incentive to lodge complaints against new firms on the most trivial grounds. Litigating the cases effectively imposes a tax on new, and typically smaller, enterprises which try to compete through advertising. How severe a tax this abuse of governmental process places on small firms is unknown.

An empirical estimation of the actual extent of this tax on new firms is probably impossible to derive. But an examination of the case load and case selection procedure may, perhaps, give a rough approximation. Current research by one of the investigators suggests that deceptive practices case selection is currently inconsistent with consumer welfare and, hence, in many respects, with the interest of competition (Baysinger and Libecap 1980). If the interests of established firms are in reducing or eliminating competition, then these findings suggest that the abuse of government process may inhibit the growth and development of small enterprise.

Another strategic practice of established firms which may have adverse impacts on the growth and development of smaller firms is the use of limit pricing. A firm with monopoly power in a given market naturally will wish to discourage entry in order to restrict market output and maintain high prices. If predatory pricing, merger, and collusion fail, the firm may choose a pricing strategy that features prices low enough to discourage entry but high enough to give some economic profit. The idea is to set a price in the market which potential entrants will find lower than their average production costs, thus, yielding them negative returns. The literature on this subject is extensive, but for the purpose of the present discussion it is sufficient to note that there is wide agreement that the practice of limit pricing, combined with other forms of strategic behavior which will be discussed later, is a viable option for established firms and can act as an artificial limit to new growth (Caves and Porter 1977; Scherer 1970, pp. 219-225). Controversy in the field is basically limited to theoretical fine points concerning the relative impacts of this strategy on consumers and competitors.

A final potential limit to new growth discussed in the literature involves a variety of exclusionary practices. This form of strategic behavior involves conduct which is not necessarily designed to destroy a rival outright, but intends to artificially foreclose certain competitive opportunities to potential or actual competitors. Examples of such behavior are the use of exclusive dealing arrangements such as requirements contracts and tying arrangements, full-line forcing, boycotts, and the creation of vertically integrated organizations. To qualify as genuine artificial limits to small firm development, such conduct must not be simply an efficient method of distribution. If it were, the behavior would have to be categorized as a natural-external barrier to growth as we discussed previously. Since many practices claimed to be exclusionary are also capable of promoting distributional and productive efficiency, the theory of exclusion is as unsettled as that of predatory pricing. A summary of the claims and counterclaims surrounding the general issue of exclusionary practices, illustrated by the example of exclusive dealing, must suffice for the present discussion.

Exclusive dealing involves an agreement between a manufacturer and a wholesaler or retailer whereby the latter devotes its efforts exclusively to the distribution of the former's output. Included in the typical arrangement is a provision prohibiting the dealer from handling the products of competing manufacturers.

Despite the fact that these contracts differ little from perfectly legal franchise agreements, they are prohibited under section 3 of the Clayton Act as being anticompetitive. The fear which may have motivated this legislation is that such arrangements would serve to artificially exclude the rivals of established manufacturers from the retail outlets they desire. While controversial, there may be some merit in this concern. Under certain circumstances, the use of exclusive dealing contracts might disrupt optimal distribution systems, and this inefficiency imposes relatively higher costs on smaller firms. If so, then the use of these arrangements by a very large firm might serve to eliminate smaller rivals (Bork 1978, pp. 156-159; Scherer 1970, pp. 509-10).

Let us assume that one manufacturer has 90 percent of the market while a smaller rival has only 10 percent and each sells its output to each of ten retailers in the same proportion as it manufacturing contribution. The larger firm might agree to sell to any given retailer only on the condition that he distribute only the large firm's goods. Such a contractual scheme might leave the smaller producer with but one retail outlet and the larger firm with the remaining nine. If the original pattern of distribution was productive, which is likely, then total production and distribution costs will rise. The costs will rise for both the large and small producer, but if the larger firm can bear the cost increase better than the smaller rival, the latter may be driven from the market (Bork 1978, p. 157). Such an outcome would make exclusive dealing an artificial-strategic barrier to growth and survival. A similar conclusion could apply to the other types of exclusionary practices listed previously. However, the field is far from settled.

Since the efficiency aspects of these practices must be taken into consideration, the question of whether existing firms will engage in inefficient contractual arrangements and vertical integrations simply to exclude potential entrants is central to the discussion. As in the case of predatory pricing, the controversy centers around the business sense of such activities.

Those unsatisfied with the conventional wisdom point out that all contracts and integrations exclude competitors. All contracts are essentially "in restraint of trade" (Bork 1978, chap. 1). Given this, the question of efficiency is paramount. Those who do not subscribe to the conventional wisdom focus on demonstrating the productive efficiency of certain "exclusionary" practices (Bork 1978, chaps. 11-15; Telser 1965, pp. 490-94; Liebeler 1979). If exclusionary practices and the foreclosure of competition represent efficient business conduct, they should be classified as natural-external limits to small firm growth, rather than as artificial-strategic constraints. The matter is far from settled at present. Therefore, judgment of whether the growth of new, smaller firms is intentionally impeded by the exclusionary practices of their larger rivals, or is merely the by-product of the efficiency of these practices, must be suspended at present. Conclusions would be out of place given the unsettled state of the literature.

Barriers to Entry

The aforementioned limits to growth were imposed in an industry by larger dominant firms against recognizable competitive targets. This rather focused sort of strategic behavior may be complemented by erecting artificial barriers to entry, which occupy a broad spectrum in the industrial organization literature. (Needham 1969, 1976; Mueller and Tilton 1969; Sherman and Willett 1967; Wenders 1971). Such barriers are not designed to attack particular rivals but, rather, are thrown up by existing firms to entrench a monopolistic position in the market and make entry by unknown competitors more difficult than would otherwise be the case. Examples of such barriers to entry are excess advertising, product differentiation, investment in excess physical production capacity to discourage entry, and limit pricing (Bain 1956; Caves and Porter 1977, pp. 245-46). The artificiality of such traditional entry barriers can be established only if efficiency is absent. For example, for promotion to be an artificial-strategic limit to growth, it must be carried beyond the point representing optimal information and distribution efforts. Excess capacity must be greater than that required to make plants or firms optimally flexible in a stochastic demand environment. These requirements open the discussion of artificial entry barriers to much the same controversy which surrounds other alleged strategic limits to growth. Once again, disagreement with conventional wisdom settles on the question of how much productive efficiency is "too much" from the point of view of small enterprises.

Promotional activities which intend to differentiate an established firm's product from the products produced by rivals (image differentiation as opposed to physical product differentiation) are considered anticompetitive in the traditional industrial organization literature. (Scherer 1970, chap. 14). Accordingly, an influential article states that "product differentiation reduces the cross-elasticity of demand between 'going' brands and the potential entrant's product and forces the entrant to make extra outlays of some sort in order to offset the 'goodwill' assets of the incumbent firms." (Caves and Porter 1977, pp. 245-46). However, Telser (1964, p. 558) found "little empirical support for an inverse association between advertising and competition, despite some plausible theorizing to the contrary." The plausible theorizing mentioned holds that firms are able to attract and hold customers on the basis of advertised advantages regardless of whether those advantages are real. As Scherer claims, "Image differentiation can . . . raise barriers to entry, increasing the likelihood that prices can be maintained continually above cost and perhaps biasing industry structure in an oligopolistic direction" (1970, p. 330). In other words, advertising can not only withhold information desired by consumers but also create false impressions causing consumers to ignore the real advantages of the products offered by the newer rivals of established firms. This is what gives image differentiation its artificial character.

The same applies to physical product differentiation, including excessive style changes, brand proliferation, and packaging proliferation. It is claimed that these practices have no other purpose than to exert hardships on smaller firms which are unable to bear the costs of such strategies. This notion of physical product differentiation as an artificial rather than natural barrier to entry is held suspect by several critics of the conventional wisdom.

To qualify as being "excessive," style changes (or brand and packaging variants, for that matter) must not be demanded by consumers at a price premium which covers these production costs. But what sorts of changes are these? If producers rapidly change style or packaging format, or produce a large number of brands of similar goods, costs will be added to consumer prices. If consumers do not desire these things, other firms are free to enter the market at lower costs and produce the optimal amount of variety, intertemporal and otherwise (Bork 1978, p. 312; McGee 1971, p. 32). Consumer preferences are treated by the proponents of the conventional wisdom as a barrier to entry, which they are. But according to this group of scholars, it is not an artificial-strategic barrier to entry. As Scherer admits, "Consumers are highly sensitive to design differences" (1970, p. 338). If the consumers' taste for variety is "excessive," then the large firm, which may enjoy an absolute cost advantage in producing variety, will outcompete its smaller rivals. Whether this represents a natural or artificial limit to growth for smaller firms is at present an unsettled question.

Heavy advertising is also believed to lead to concentrated industries. If that were true, it would be evidence that such advertising can differentiate, in the minds of consumers, a particular product from the products of potentially lower cost competitors and induce the consumers to pay higher prices for perfect substitutes. This is a form of unjustified goodwill enjoyed by the larger firms which can engage in relatively more advertising (Scherer 1970, p. 341; Comaner and Wilson 1967; Williamson 1963). As indicated previously, there are certain scale economies associated with advertising which allow larger advertisers to differentiate their products in the minds of consumers at lower unit costs. This is a natural limit to growth; whether or not a firm would rationally engage in excess advertising as an anti-competitive weapon is, however, an unproven hypothesis. As Scherer concluded, "It appears that advertising expenditures may gravitate toward slightly higher levels in oligopolistic than in atomistically structured industries, ceteris paribus, but the relationship is weak and erratic" (1970, p. 342).

Moreover, the ability to compete means the ability to deal with the market environment as one finds it. If consumers prefer products which have been differentiated through advertising, success may hinge upon filling this need. As Bork notes, "When consumers prefer the differentiated product and hence make output restriction possible, they have shown that they prefer the higher price for that product to a lower price for a standardized product" (1978, p. 313). The firm which is unable to compete in the differentiation game may have to accept this as a fact of life given by consumer preference patterns rather than strategic behavior on the part of large firms.

The predatory use of excess capacity may also be treated as an artificial-strategic limit to new growth. The use of capital requirements as an anticompetitive weapon requires that established firms, or groups of such firms, act in concert to expand their physical capacity beyond what is efficient. Such a strategy will force potential entrants to come into the market with larger amounts of capital than they would otherwise need. For example, established firms may vertically integrate in order to foreclose new competition. A producer of shoes who buys a shoe retailer supposedly creates a barrier to entry since all new entrants into the shoe business must compete on both the manufacturing and retailing levels (Blake and Jones 1965, p. 377; Caves and Porter 1977, p. 246).

Established firms may also build excess capacity in anticipation of future market demand growth. As that increase in demand materializes, they will be in a position to supply the market quickly and, thereby, foreclose new entry (Wilcox and Shepherd 1975, p. 209). Finally, incumbent market leaders may use excess capacity to reinforce the effect of a limit-pricing strategy. According to Caves and Porter, "Unused production capacity makes credible a threat of price warfare against entrant firms . . . investment in the excess capacity to retaliate might pay whether or not it is ever used" (1977, p. 245). Some of these assertions about the strategic use of capacity as an artificial entry barrier clearly have merit and suggest an artificial limit to growth.

However, the use of excess capacity as an anticompetitive weapon is difficult for some commentators to accept since, by its nature, it places established firms at a cost disadvantage relative to firms investing only in the efficient amount of physical plant and distribution facilities. In other words, to be an artificial barrier to entry, the capacity expansion (either internal or through merger), by definition, cannot increase the efficiency (in the short-run or over a longer planning horizon) of the incumbent firm. If efficiency is not thereby increased, the costs of the incumbent firm will be higher, thus, raising the minimum profit-maximizing price and attracting new entry by firms which have not burdened themselves with wasteful plants or integrated divisions (Bork 1978, pp. 241, 320-24; McGee 1971, p. 51). The only exception to this is the use of limit entry pricing which is clearly an explicit strategy to keep rivals from encroaching on the established firm's market-shares. (Sherer 1970, pp. 216-20). The strategy involves setting a price below the level required for full short-run profit maximization but above the level expected to induce entry by new or existing firms. This is clearly a type of artificial limit to the growth of small firms and a potentially rational business strategy for larger firms. The literature on the subject is vast and complex, but the general conclusion is that the use of limit pricing to deter entry can impede the growth of small firms in a market.

The conclusion that strategic inefficiency is illogical and, hence, unlikely does not necessarily apply to a dynamic consideration of the problem. The use of excess capacity in combination with a history of predatory price cutting may serve as a strategic limit to new growth. Whether or not such conduct exists and is effective is an empirical question since no logical argument against this assertion exists in the literature. In all, the question of whether excess capacity represents an artificial or natural barrier to new growth remains unsettled.

A Caveat to the Artificial Limit to Growth Literature

A final note to this chapter is that it is not clear that the question of whether or not small firms face strategic artificial barriers to new growth can be completely resolved by the application of economic logic alone. We know that large established firms have the incentive to erect the barriers discussed in this section in order to more effectively restrict output. The same applies to the use of abusive trade practices and foreclosure tactics. A general criticism of the conventional wisdom may be found in the fact that such behaviors, if they occur, are the decisions not of the firms but of the manager of firms. This suggests that organization considerations play a role in determining the logic of such conduct. For most industries the use of artificial restraints on entry requires a strategic decision by hired corporate managers who must choose to forego current profits in order to reap long-term returns in excess of the competitive level. This wealth maximizing behavior might be expected from owner-managers, but is less likely to be the behavior of a hired manager in the organizational environment of corporate enterprise where ownership and management are distinct (Berle and Means 1968). This conclusion holds regardless of the strength of one's attachment to the Berle and Means hypothesis that the hired managers of large corporations are free to pursue their own interests without complete regard for the interests of their firm's owners.

Let us assume first that the separation of ownership and control hypothesis is basically weak, which is an assumption supported by a vast and growing literature that argues that there are a variety of market constraints on managerial conduct which assure a close correspondence between managerial utility and stockholder wealth (Johnson 1978, pp. 77-126). If hired corporate managers are induced to maximize profits because of certain market forces which punish deviant behavior, then artificial-strategic entry barriers may be in the long-term interest of the stockholders, but not in the short-term interests of managers. The central question raised here is whether or not the capital markets can accurately evaluate the wealth impacts of certain predatory strategic behavior. That is, if managers engage in anticompetitive behavior, such as *excess* capacity expansion, image differentiation, physical product differentiation, vertical integration, and the like, will the capital markets react to the necessary short-term fall off in performance favorably or adversely? There is no reason to believe, at present, that the capital markets will react favorably since the behaviors involved are the sort of thing managers would want to hide. One cannot advertise the long-term strategic advantages of such conduct to the capital markets without also advertising the same to the antitrust authorities.

It may be the case that such artificial-strategic barriers are only feasible for firms managed by individuals who can safely ignore the impact of such conduct on current market values and, hence, managerial tenure. These would be owner-managers who are, in fact, rare in the large enterprises most likely to try to engage in such activity.

But what if the separation-of-ownership-and-control theme does not accurately describe corporate reality? If so, then the hired managers of large corporations need not be overly concerned with stockholder welfare. But if this is the case, why would hired managers engage in strategic behavior if the goal of such behavior is to increase the value of the firm (wealth of stockholders) over the long haul? Managers can engage in many activities more attractive than building up artificial barriers to new competition, especially since such activity, by definition, reduces current returns which the managers could capture in the form of nonpecuniary income. One must always remember that those who claim that large firms can erect artificial barriers to entry or engage in abusive trade practices do so in order to maximize the wealth of the firm, which means the wealth of the stockholders. If ownership and control are separated, the chief motivation for such behavior is absent. Until the internal organizational problems associated with artificial-strategic limits to growth are resolved, the question of whether small firms really suffer from such conduct cannot be established by the fact that an owner-managed firm would find them advantageous.

In summary, this chapter has discussed several artificial-strategic barriers to the growth of new and smaller firms. Of all the limits-to-growth categories discussed in this book the artificial-strategic limits literature is the least settled. This suggests that public policy remedies directed at these potential sources of growth retardation be applied with great care. Until more is known about the feasibility of such anticompetitive practices as discussed above, any policy aimed at "correcting" them is as likely to do harm as good.

7

State and Federal Regulations as Cost Barriers to New Entry

Federal securities law and state blue-sky (securities) laws were enacted to protect investors from the predations of unscrupulous operators in the securities markets. Ultimately, legislative interest resided in a desire to stimulate capital formation by providing a safe market environment for capital investors. However, an unintended by-product of the securities laws has been the erection of an artificial barrier to entry for small or new enterprises seeking to issue securities in order to raise development capital. To the extent that these regulations impose differentially higher costs on small business, the economic and political advantages of small firms are frustrated.

Economists generally agree that the greatest protection of consumers is found in free markets where open competition exists among firms. A necessary and sufficient condition for such competition is the existence of free entry, which simply means the expansion of productive capacity, either by de novo establishment of new firms or by capital expansions of existing firms. Monopoly, on the other hand, is defined as a situation in which an industry fails to expand its capacity through entry, when such expansion is justified by the existing cost-and-demand situation. Since it takes into consideration the adverse consequences of monopoly, public policy (such as the antitrust law), which is in the interest of promoting competition and, hence, of promoting consumer welfare is supposed to prevent artificial barriers to new entry. Unfortunately, federal and state regulations of new securities issues restrict the entry of new capital into other businesses, especially small businesses, by public stock offerings. Hence, as discussed in part in chapter 5, these laws may discriminate against the formation of small businesses.

Securities laws serve as a regressive tax on new business organizations, thereby punishing the smallest publicly organized firms and discouraging would-be business promoters from entering into competition with larger existing corporations. The results are a bias toward fewer small firms and an increase in the size of existing larger firms. In particular, merit regulations of blue-sky laws serve as a deterrent to organizing small firms. These rules discriminate in favor of existing firms and the wealthy by public offerings of shares of stock in enterprises being organized or expanded. Blue-sky laws provisions will be shown, in conjunction with federal security regulations, to cause the outright prohibition of the organization of some enterprises by monetary discrimination against smaller firms.

Effects of Regulations

Federal and state securities regulations are structured so that if one wished to offer securities in a venture to the public, the securities must comply with the provisions of federal securities laws and the securities laws in every state in which the stock will be sold. Since federal and state registration provisions are very complex and the laws of the states vary (as will be explained later in the chapter), a general model of security laws will be used here to explain the anticompetitive effects of such laws.

Securities can be exempt from registration if the offering is made to a small number of individuals, to individuals of a certain wealth and investment sophistication, and under a certain dollar limitation. However, if one wishes to raise more capital than is practical under the exemptions, then the securities must be registered at the state and federal levels. Hence, wealthy entrepreneurs with investment knowledge benefit more by the exemptions from registration than do small entrepreneurs, who usually have less cash at the start and require more contributors to the venture.

The cost of registration is enormous when viewed in the context of the smaller enterprises. A study in 1970 showed that attorney fees generally range from twenty-five thousand dollars to fifty thousand dollars for registration with the Securities and Exchange Commission alone; compliance with blue-sky laws increases the fees (Schneider and Manko 1970). Printing expenses for the presentation of the offering to the SEC and state officials are twenty thousand dollars at the minimum. There are also accounting expenses which run into considerable dollar sums. Since expenses typically ranged from seventy thousand dollars to one hundred thousand dollars for small offerings in 1970, these costs have probably more than doubled because of inflation.

All of the services one must purchase to satisfy registration provisions are procured in the competitive market. Hence, the fact that small offerings will incur a higher cost proportionally than do the larger offerings does not reflect discrimination on the part of the producers of such services. It merely represents the fact that there are certain minimum costs which every public offering must incur, regardless of the size of the offering. For offerings under $0.5 million, these expenses ("Other Expenses") run about 10 percent of the value of the total offering. Whereas, as shown in table 7-1, the expenses only run about 1 percent of the value of the total offering when it is in the $20 million range. These figures only reflect the cost of complying with federal regulations. The cost of compliance with state blue-sky regulations adds additional expense in line with the same general distribution of costs in which the greatest costs proportionally fall on the smallest enterprises.

There are scale economies in the production of large offerings. This is evidenced by the cost pattern of the compensation received by underwriters of security issues. These services are provided competitively within the

Table 7-1
Registration Expenses by Size of Offering, 1971-1972

Size of Issue (Millions)	Number	Compensation (Percent of Gross Proceeds)	Other Expenses (Percent of Gross Proceeds)
Under .5	43	13.24	10.35
.5-.99	227	12.48	8.26
1.0-1.99	271	10.60	5.87
2.0-4.99	450	8.19	3.71
5.0-9.99	287	6.70	2.03
10.0-19.99	170	5.52	1.11
20.0-49.99	109	4.41	.62
50.0-99.99	30	3.94	.31
100.0-499.99	12	3.03	.16
Over 500.00	0	—	—
Total/Averages	1599	8.41	4.02

Source: Securities and Exchange Commission, *Cost of Flotation of Registered Issues 1971-72*, December 1974, p. 9.

regulatory guidelines about who may underwrite offerings, and display that the larger the offering the lower the percent of the value of the offering absorbed by that expense. The distribution of the costs of underwriting issues also demonstrated that larger offerings usually are less risky than many of the small offerings, so the larger organizations are charged a lower insurance premium.

These costs should be compared to the distribution of costs that might be incurred if registration were not required. This is illustrated in figure 7-1, which displays the costs of a public offering of different sizes under the current federal registration provisions and the costs that might be incurred without registration requirements. What the curve would be is not known. However, there generally would be lower legal fees, accounting fees, and printing expenses. As a percent of the value of the offering, it is clear that the savings would be proportionally greatest for the smaller enterprises. As illustrated in figure 7-1, if the costs were, say, half of what they are under the current registration provisions, then the benefit of the removal of registration would be greatest for small organizations. Hence, securities regulation effectively serves as a regressive tax on the organization of enterprises. The smaller the enterprise, the higher the "tax rate" on the organization.

From public finance theory it is clear what the basic effects of such a regressive tax are. Fewer businesses will come into existence with the registration expenses than without them. However, since the effect is

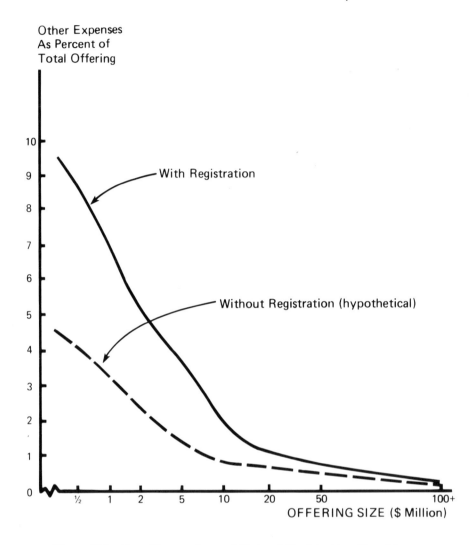

Figure 7-1. Cost Comparison of Federal Registration Provisions

regressive, fewer small businesses than large businesses will be organized under the present registration rules.

For firms which do come into existence (pay the high registration costs), the costs (the tax) are borne by the promoters and the purchasers of the securities. Although there may be dispute as to the final incidence of such a tax, the effect is clear. A number of potential entrants have been barred from the market.

In several decisions the Supreme Court has made it clear that one of the goals of antitrust law is to prevent barriers to entry into industry. The court has noted the importance of *potential competitors* in helping to insure competition (see, for example, *FTC* v. *Proctor Gamble Co.,* 386 U.S. 568, 1967). The economic sense of these decisions is not debated here; rather, the point is that the security laws, by raising the costs faced by new entrants, reduce potential competition. Whereas, without existing registration procedures, promoters may be induced to enter an industry when they project, say, a 10 percent rate-of-return; because of the entry costs they may require the projection of, say, a 20 percent rate-of-return. This means that existing competitors can earn above normal rates-of-return before there is a challenge to their market positions by potential competitors.

Once the rate-of-return in a certain industry is above normal, existing firms will have an incentive to increase production to capture the expanding market. There is considerable debate as to whether or not such intraindustry competition will keep the rate-of-return normal. Whether it does or not, it is clear that the industry will tend to be more concentrated than if it faced a greater degree of external competition.

State securities merit regulations are designed in an attempt to lessen the investment risk for investors in newly promoted firms. Proponents claim that because no organized market exists to reflect past performance as with seasoned stocks, the securities of new organizations are too speculative and, therefore, require direct government regulation beyond registration and disclosure rules. Merit regulations add to the risks faced by promoters of new businesses, especially the relatively small firm.

As discussed in detail later in the chapter, merit regulations take the form of rules:

1. Regulating the maximum expenses of public offerings;
2. Requiring a minimum equity investment by promoters;
3. Regulating the price that insiders must pay for their stock relative to the proposed price for public investors;
4. Regulating securities offering prices in relation to earnings ratios;
5. Regulating the amount of warrants and options granted of officers, key employees and underwriters;
6. Establishing minimal shareholder voting rights; and
7. Regulating interest and dividend coverage with respect to senior securities.

There is little empirical evidence of the effectiveness of merit regulations. It appears that merit regulation fails to perform its appointed tasks (Mofsky and Tollison, 1977). That topic aside, the anticompetitive effects of merit regulations are unambiguous.

Provisions of State Securities Laws

During the 1910s most states adopted securities regulations, generally called blue-sky laws in reference to worthless securities that had been sold with nothing more substantive behind them than the blue sky. After the stock market crash of 1929, it was believed that federal regulation was necessary to supplement the state laws, which were thought to have been ineffective in preventing securities abuses uncovered prior to the passage of the 1933 and 1934 federal securities laws. A uniform state security statue has been adopted, with some modifications, in over half of the states; in the other states there is great variety in the scope of their securities regulations.

Table 7-2 provides a relatively easy way to compare the state securities laws and merit rules. The table headings (numbers) are explained in the text, which also explains the categories reported in the body of the table and the qualifications of some entries. There is considerable diversity in state securities laws, primarily with respect to how they affect offerings by small or new businesses. The effect in the strict states is to raise the costs of using the public equity markets of the promoters of such enterprises. Whether the costs that are imposed on such promoters, and the cost to consumers in reduced competition, outweigh the value of the protection to investors has not been determined by any investor.

Table 7-2
Provisions of State Securities Laws as of 1978

State	1	2	3	4	5	6	7	8	9	10
Alabama	Y	AB	UA	10	—	10	I	R	2	2
Alaska	Y	AB	UA	10	—	20	I	R	1	2
Arizona	Y	AB	—	10	10	35+	I	—	3	3
Arkansas	Y	AB	UA	10	—	25	I	R	3	2
California	Y	AB	UA	10	5*	5 –	I	—	2	2
Colorado	Y	AB	UA	25	—	35+	I	R	2	2
Connecticut	N	—	—	—	—	35+	—	—	—	—
Delaware	Y	AB	UA	10	—	25	I	R	1	2
District of Columbia	N	—	—	—	—	35+	—	—	—	—
Florida	Y	AB	—	25	25	20+	I	—	2	2
Georgia	Y	B*	—	10	10	25+	I	—	3	1
Hawaii	Y	AB	UA	25	25	25	I	R	3	2
Idaho	Y	AB	UA	10	—	10	I	R	1	2
Illinois	Y	AB	—	25	25	25+	I	—	3	3
Indiana	Y	AB	UA	10	—	20	I	R	3	2
Iowa	Y	AB	—	20	20*	20+	I	—	2	3
Kansas	Y	AB	UA	U	15	—	I	R	3	2
Kentucky	Y	AB	UA	10	—	10	I	R	2	2
Louisiana	Y	AB	—	U	—	25	I	—	2	2
Maine	Y	AB	—	10	10	10 –	—	—	2	3
Maryland	Y	AB	UA	10	—	35+	I	R	3	2

Table 7-2 *(continued)*

State	1	2	3	4	5	6	7	8	9	10
Massachusetts	Y	AB	UA	10	—	25	I	R	2	2
Michigan	Y	AB	UA	10	10	15	I	R	2	2
Minnesota	Y	AB	—	10	5-25*	25+	I	—	2	2
Mississippi	Y	AB	—	10	10	10-	I	—	2	3
Missouri	Y	AB	UA	10	25	15+	I	R	1	2
Montana	Y	AB	UA	10	—	10	I	R	1	2
Nebraska	Y	AB	UA	10	—	10	I	R	2	2
Nevada	Y	B	—	10	—	25	—	—	2	1
New Hampshire	Y	AB	—	—	—	—	—	R-	2	3
New Jersey	Y	B*	—	10	—	8-10	I	R	2	1
New Mexico	Y	AB	UA	15	25	25-	I	R	3	2
New York	Y	B	—	—	—	10	—	R-	2	1
North Carolina	Y	AB	—	25	—	25	I	—	2	3
North Dakota	Y	AB	—	15	—	10	I	—	2	3
Ohio	Y	AB	—	U	5	5-	—	—	2	2
Oklahoma	Y	AB	UA	10	—	25+	I	R	3	2
Oregon	Y	AB	—	10	10	25-	I	R-	2	2
Pennsylvania	Y	AB	UA	5*	5*	25+	I	R	1	2
Puerto Rico	Y	AB	UA	10*	10*	10	I	R	2	2
Rhode Island	Y	AB	—	—	—	—	I	—	2	3
South Carolina	Y	AB	UA	10	—	25	I	R	2	2
South Dakota	Y	AB	—	U	—	—	I	R-	3	3
Tennessee	Y	AB	—	30	30	15	I	—	3	3
Texas	Y	AB	—	25	25	25-	I	R	2	2
Utah	Y	AB	UA	10	10	—	I	R	3	2
Vermont	Y	AB	—	25	25	25-	I	—	2	3
Virginia	Y	AB	—	30	30	30-	I	R	2	2
Washington	Y	AB	UA	10	—	20	I	R	1	2
West Virginia	Y	AB	—	—	—	35+	I	—	2	3
Wisconsin	Y	AB	UA	U	15	10-15-	I	R	2	2
Wyoming	Y	AB	UA	15	—	15	I	R	2	2

Explanation of Provisions

1. Does the state require securities to be sold in that state to be registered with a state securities commission? Y = Yes, N = No. In Connecticut and the District of Columbia, the only states not requiring registration, securities dealers do have to be registered. Lack of securities registration means that the states rely on federal securities registration.

2. Of the states requiring securities registration, which require the registration of interstate securities (A) and/or intrastate securities (B)? AB = interstate and intrastate securities registered, A = interstate securities only, B = intrastate securities only. New Jersey requires the filing of SEC registration materials, and, upon reading those registration materials, can prohibit the sale of interstate securities in the state, so

there is de facto interstate registration; similarly, Georgia requires the filing of a Notice of Intent to sell interstate securities. New York and New Jersey have separate registration requirements for real estate syndication offerings.

3. Has the state substantially adopted the Uniform Securities Act (UA)? UA = state has adopted Uniform Securities Act. Section 402(a) of the UA provides exemption from registration for the following: securities issued or guaranteed by a governmental unit of the United States or Canada; securities issued by a bank, savings institution, trust company, credit union, or similar institution organized under and supervised by the laws of the federal and/or state government; securities issued by nonprofit corporations (religious, educational, charitable, fraternal, social, athletic, reformatory, chamber of commerce, or trade or professional group) which operate solely for such purpose; short-term commercial paper issued in connection with current transactions; securities issued by certain cooperatives; and investment contracts issued on connection with employee stock purchase, savings, pension, profit sharing, or a similar plan. Many non-UA states have similar provisions. UA states and several other states exempt securities approved for listing on major stock exchanges. With a minor exception in Nevada, all states exempt securities listed on the New York Stock Exchange. All except Michigan exempt stock listed on the American Stock Exchange. Most, but not all, states provide exemptions for securities listed on other exchanges like the Midwest Stock Exchange and the Pacific Coast Stock Exchange. In California, the structure of the exemption essentially allows stocks listed on the NYSE and AMEX to be exempt, but not others.

4. How many preorganization subscriptions may be made without registration? In general, preorganization subscriptions are used to line up financing in advance of implementing the proposed venture. Registration may be required when the securities are actually issued, but exemption from registration at the time of the preorganization helps to reduce the costs of launching a venture. The numbers listed for the states in this provision are the limits on the number of subscribers allowed under the preorganization exemption. In many states, the limited offering exemptions, provision 6, will be more useful than this provision. U means an unlimited number of preorganizational subscriptions are allowed. In most cases these subscriptions must be made without advertising or the use of commissions for the procuring of the subscriptions.

5. How many subscribers could contribute funds to the corporation (pay for their stock) before registration would be required? The maximum number is shown for those states which allow receipt of payment. In

most of these states this can serve the same purpose as the limited offering exemption, provision 6. California requires some filings and places other restrictions on this form of payment for stock that limits its usefulness. Iowa requires all sales completed under this provision to be reported within thirty days of the sale. Minnesota has different sets of requirements under different exemption provisions. The exemption grows less useful as the number of subscribers goes over five. Pennsylvania and Puerto Rico have such stringent requirements that the provision is generally useless.

6. If limited offerings (private placement) are allowed without registration, how many stockholders may there be without their having to register? The number for the states which allows for this provision is provided. Most UA states allow for a specific number of offers to be made within twelve months. No commissions may be paid, and the issuer must believe that the buyers desire the stock for investment purposes. The states where the number is followed by a + sign are the ones that set the number of sales that may be made rather than the number of offers. This is sometimes limited by a maximum number of offers too, but, in general, it is a more generous provision. The states where the number is followed by a − sign are the ones in which the exemption is lost if, as stock trades hands, the number of total stockholders ever associated with the company ever reaches the statutory maximum. California and Ohio have additional filing requirements. Maine, Mississippi, Vermont, and Wisconsin limit this provision to domestic corporations. The states allowing thirty-five purchasers essentially follow the SEC rules on private placement (Rule 146).

7. Does the state allow an exemption from registration for private placements made only to institutional investors who hold the stock only for investment purposes? If so, the state has an I.

8. Does the state have the UA provision that exempts from registration certain rights' offerings? If so, the state has an R to indicate that it allows this exemption which helps to lower the organization costs for a new stock issue. Oregon, New Hampshire, New York, and South Dakota have very limited versions of this exemption, so they are classified with an R−.

9. How stringent are the state's registration-by-coordination provisions with respect to Regulation A offerings? For states rated with a 1, the state law is more lenient than the SEC requirements in this regard, which generally means that less information is required. For states rated 2, the

information requirements are the same as those of the SEC. For states rated 3, the information requirements are more costly than the federal requirements. Many states have lower registration requirements for seasoned companies, which is an obvious advantage for existing larger firms.

10. How are the state registration requirements aligned with SEC registration requirements? In the four easiest states, rated 1, if a security is registered with the SEC, it is exempt from state rules. In most of the states, rated 2, while there must be state registration, there is registration by coordination with SEC registration. In the most stringent states, rated 3, state registration beyond SEC registration requirements are not coordinated, so it is more costly.

Merit Regulations

Table 7-3 concerns the merit provisions of state securities laws. Unlike federal securities laws, which set informational requirements that must be met to receive approval to market a security, some states set qualitative requirements that must be met before the security may be sold. In some states these requirements are set by statute. An offerer must meet the statutory guidelines with respect to how much stock he may sell himself, at what price, what expenses may be incurred, and so forth. In other states, the statute sets guidelines that are interpreted by the state securities commissioner on a case-by-case basis. This is generally believed to result in discrimination against offerings that are small and/or are being promoted by an organization or promoter with little track record. Because the commissioners are less certain about the likelihood of success for such promoters, they set stricter requirements for them than are set for more "seasoned" offerings. The requirements may be set so that they are simply impossible to meet.

No good empirical study has been done of the impact of such state laws. The primary problem is the lack of data. Most states do not collect and maintain annual data on securities approved and rejected or on the terms set for approval; further, it is very difficult to track the progress of all the offerings approved, or, if they are disapproved, to discover what happened to the enterprise or proposed enterprise. In some cases an alternative source of financing may be found; in other cases, the proposal is taken to a more sympathetic state for approval. Unfortunately, such information is only based on the observations of securities practitioners since comprehensive studies have not been performed.

Table 7-3
Merit Provisions of State Securities Laws as of 1978

State	11	12	13	14	15	16	17	18	19	20	21
Alabama	2	15	33	50	1	3	—	—	2	1	—
Alaska	2	15	25	50	2	3	15+	1	3	1	—
Arizona	2	5	—	—	0	3	—	—	2	—	—
Arkansas	2	10	33	—	2	3	13	2	3	1	—
California	3	10	25	—	2	3	15	2	3	1	—
Colorado	1	10	25	25	2	3	20	2	1	1	—
Connecticut	0	—	—	—	—	—	—	—	—	—	—
Delaware	2	—	—	—	0	—	—	—	2	—	—
District of Columbia	0	—	—	—	—	—	—	—	—	—	—
Florida	3	15	15	—	2	2	—	2	—	1	1
Georgia	2	—	—	—	0	2	15	—	1	—	—
Hawaii	2	—	33	—	1	3	15	—	1	—	2
Idaho	2	10	—	—	2	3	15	—	1	1	1
Illinois	2	15	33	—	2	—	15+	—	—	—	—
Indiana	2	10	—	—	2	2	1	1	2	1	1
Iowa	2	10	—	—	1	3	15	1	—	1	1
Kansas	2	10	33	—	2	3	15	2	3	1	—
Kentucky	2	10	33	50	1	3	15	1	2	1	2
Louisiana	3	15	33	—	2	3	15	1	2	1	—
Maine	2	—	—	—	—	—	—	—	—	—	—
Maryland	2	—	—	—	—	—	—	—	—	—	—
Massachusetts	2	—	25	—	0	2	18+	—	—	—	—
Michigan	2	15	33	—	1	3	15+	—	3	—	—
Minnesota	2	15	33+	—	2	3	15	—	2	—	—
Mississippi	2	10	10	—	2	—	—	—	1	—	1
Missouri	3	15	50	50	1	3	17	1	2	—	—
Montana	2	—	—	—	2	3	1	—	2	—	1
Nebraska	1	10	—	—	2	1	1	—	2	—	—
Nevada	2	5	—	—	—	—	20	—	—	—	—
New Hampshire	2	—	—	—	—	—	—	—	—	—	—
New Jersey	1	—	—	—	0	1	1	—	2	—	—
New Mexico	2	10	—	—	—	3	20	—	2	1	—
New York	1	—	—	—	—	—	—	—	—	—	—
North Carolina	3	—	—	—	—	—	10+	—	—	—	—
North Dakota	3	10	—	—	2	3	15+	—	2	—	—
Ohio	2	10	—	—	2	2	15	—	—	1	—
Oklahoma	2	10	33	—	2	3	20	—	2	—	—
Oregon	3	—	—	—	—	2	1	—	2	—	—
Pennsylvania	2	—	—	—	0	2	—	—	2	—	—
Puerto Rico	2	—	—	—	2	2	1	—	2	—	—
Rhode Island	2	—	—	—	—	—	—	—	—	—	—
South Carolina	2	—	100	100	2	1	20	—	1	—	2
South Dakota	3	10	25	—	1	3	15	2	1	1	1
Tennessee	2	—	—	—	2	—	15	1	—	—	—
Texas	2	10	—	—	2	—	20	2	1	—	—
Utah	2	10	33	—	2	2	20	—	2	1	1
Vermont	3	—	—	—	—	—	—	—	—	—	—
Virginia	2	—	—	—	—	—	—	—	—	—	—
Washington	2	10	50	—	2	3	1	—	1	1	—
West Virginia	3	10	—	100	2	3	20	2	—	1	1
Wisconsin	2	10	25	—	1	2	15	1	2	1	1
Wyoming	2	10	33	—	1	3	20	—	2	—	—

Explanation of Provisions

11. How stringent are the state merit regulations? States with 0 have no merit rules because they do not register securities; states with 1 have limited merit rules; states with 2 have UA formalized rules; and states with 3 have non-UA provisions which generally give great latitude to the securities commissioners on the basis of "fairness."

12. Does the state require promoters to purchase a certain percent of the stock they wish to promote? The table shows the percent minimum ownership requirement of the states with such specific rules. Some states have indefinite percentages; in practices they are probably in the same general range.

13. How much stock dilution does the state allow? The percentages in the table show how much stock the promoter is allowed to buy at a bargain rate for himself. The higher the percent, the less the incentive to promote a new stock corporation. Minnesota ranges from 33 to 60 percent.

14. What kind of price restrictions are placed on cheap stocks? The figures in the table are the mandated percent of the stock offering price that promoters must pay for their stock. The higher the percent, the more restrictive. Many of the states with no number allow the commissioners to exercise their discretion in the matter, so the net effect may be somewhat strict in some cases.

15. The standards of options and warrants for underwriters—do they follow certain guidelines, allow the commissioners to do as they think best, or is there no control? In states with 0, the regulations are not specific; the regulators do as they think best (whether this makes it more difficult than the next two options is unknown). In states with a 1, they follow the rules of the Midwest Securities Commissioners Association, which are a bit more flexible (but not much) than the rules of the North American Securities Administrators which are followed by states with a 2. Other states appear to have no controls.

16. Does the state control promotional/cheap stock by requiring the stock to be in escrow in some manner until the company has achieved a certain financial status? Those states with such rules were given a 1 if they only have the UA provision, a 2 if they give the commissioners discretion over the matter (which can result in very stringent controls in some instances), and a 3 if they have more requirements specified in the law beyond categories 1 and 2. Again, compliance with these rules tends to be most

difficult for a new or small company. Existing larger firms easily meet the requirements in most cases.

17. Does the state regulate the amount of the offering that can be spent on underwriting commissions and selling expenses? If not, nothing is reported. A 1 is listed for states that allow "reasonable" commissions and expenses, and the actual percent maximum is given for states that establish the number. A + is added to the states in which the percent only applies to commissions; they allow other selling expenses too.

18. Does the state control the offering price of new securities? In most states, no, but in the other states that do, some (1) set the price earnings ratio. In most states the highest the P/E can be is 25, although it is 35 in Iowa, unless an exception is granted by the commissioners. In the other states that control the price of the stock (2), the price must be approved by the commissioners. Bloomenthal states that "these and other regulations relating to the offering price are generally drawn so as to exclude new companies or companies in the promotional stage . . ." (1978, pp. 14-43). This means that these regulations can be used to kill new offerings at the whim of the securities commissioners. As one might expect, the Midwest Securities Commissioners Association has been pushing for the adoption of such rules, so as to expand the role of the state commissioner in new offerings.

19. Are state securities commissioners empowered to require proceeds from stock sales to be impounded until certain financial conditions are met? The states that have such controls, which again make it more difficult to sell new stocks in small companies, are given a 1 if they have the rules but are apparently less stringent because they allow commissioners and expenses to be paid out of the impounded funds. They are given a 2 if they have the usual impounding of funds at the discretion of the commissioners. They are given a 3 if the funds must be impounded until the end of the transaction, and no commissions or expenses may be paid until that time from these funds. These rules generally only apply if best-effort underwriting is used, where the stock is not necessarily sold as in the case of firm commitment underwriting.

20. Does the state restrict or prohibit the use of nonvoting stock for new stock issues? A 1 is listed for the states which have such restrictions, which generally do not affect larger, established companies selling stock.

21. Is there a restriction on the use of preferred stock? The states which prohibit or restrict the use of preferred stock and debt securities are listed with a 1; states which place minor limits on the use of debt securities

are listed with a 2. Again, these restrictions generally only apply to new, small stock issuances.

Effect of Offering Regulations

The state security requirements impose some cost on potential promoters, or require that promoters meet some criteria set by the state for promoted enterprises that will be funded via public equity capital markets. Consider the effects of some of the requirements of some laws.

The requirements that promoters must contribute some percent of the total offering again acts as a tax on offerings and clearly discriminates against promoters who are not wealthy or cannot get a wealthy person to sponsor the offering. For example, in Florida promoters must put up 15 percent of the total value of the offering. Hence, for a $1 million offering, the promoters must put up $150,000. This money must be in escrow for two years, so the promoter must be able to have sufficient funds to absorb the costs of having idle funds for that length of time. This requirement acts as a tax on new business promotions, just as registration requirements do, and acts as a deterrent to nonwealthy individuals. Even if a promoter can find a wealthy sponsor willing to put up the cash, the sponsor will be able to extract most of the gain for himself. Thus, nonwealthy individuals with good business promotions will be required to bargain away some of the gains from their entrepreneurial talents. Again, the effect is to discriminate in favor of the wealthy and in favor of established businesses.

The limit on the offering price per share to a ratio of the price paid by the promoters acts in much the same manner as does the cash requirement just discussed. By this rule, in order for a promoter to maintain control of the business being promoted, he will have to have sufficient cash to purchase stock at a price deemed to be "fair" by the merit regulators. If he does not have sufficient cash to purchase the stock, then sufficient funds must be obtained from a source wealthy enough to cover the needed expenses. The source will, of course, be able to bargain away from the promoter some of the profits which would have accrued to him otherwise. This has the effect of placing a tax on less wealthy promoters, discouraging the number of small business promotions, and favoring big business promotions and expansion by existing firms.

The net effect of these constraints is to prevent many potential offerings from being successful or from even being attempted. In some states the merit rules are interpreted to require offering expenses to be so low as a percent of the offering that it is simply impossible to meet the rule (Mofsky 1972). In these cases, the laws serve as a complete bar to small offerings within some states. As mentioned before, security commissioners are often placed in the position of ruling on whether or not a proposed offering should be allowed. It is simply wishful thinking to expect such officials, no matter how diligent they may be in doing their job, to be better at predicting the success of new enterprises than are the promoters and those who would volunteer to finance their ventures. The efficient market hypothesis has dispelled the idea that anyone can predict the future success of an enterprise better than other similarly informed individuals.

Of course, the purpose of the blue-sky laws is to promote investor confidence, which should increase capital formation in new firms. However, there is no empirical support for this proposition. Mofsky and Tollison, reviewing the literature, found that the performance of firms which have and have not been registered by states under blue-sky laws did not differ statistically (1977). In other words, investor welfare has not been affected favorably by merit regulation. As noted in chapter 5, studies by Professor Stigler and others have cast doubt on the usefulness of federal securities regulations. If this is the case, only the anticompetitive costs of such regulations remain.

In sum, the costs of security regulations are enormous. Most of the costs are imposed on small business promoters, who are either forced out of the market or are forced to sell future gains they otherwise would have received for their talents. The long run effect is to stifle entrepreneurial efforts, which prevents less wealthy individuals from advancing in the business world as rapidly as they would have if they were wealthy at the start. The other costs are borne by consumers. They have lost an important source of competition among the firms and potential firms which service them. As Professor Mofsky has observed, "No empirical study has examined the extent to which the Blue Sky Laws have contributed to decreasing the total number of new businesses being developed in our economic system. But in the absence of reliable data, there is no more basis for concluding that the number is insignificant than there is for concluding that the number is substantial" (1977, pp. 20-21).

8

The Experience Curve Phenomenon—A Consequence of Growth

One of the most widely discussed concepts in business research has been the experience curve phenomenon. This concept has extensive implications for a number of fields including strategic management, marketing, production management, finance, microeconomics, and public policy. The experience curve phenomenon was hypothesized initially through research completed by staff members of the Boston Consulting Group. This research, reported originally in *Perspectives on Experience* (1968), focused on the relationship between accumulated product experience (production volume), costs, prices, and market-share for thirteen products in various industries. The Boston Consulting Group (BCG) argued that the findings concerning the experience curve possessed implications which extended far beyond the previously recognized learning curve (Andress 1954; Hirshmann 1964). Rather than simply predicting the relationship between production volume and labor costs, the BCG contended that the relationship applied to "the full range of costs including development, capital distribution and overhead as well as labor costs."

In the years since the original explanation of this concept, the field of strategic management has built on this "early" empirical study. It has served as the basis for theory and research, and it has been the object of controversy. As such, it is appropriate at this time to review the experience curve and its implications, discuss the literature that relates to it, and engage in a critical analysis of it. This chapter does not purport to include all of the complex issues affiliated with the experience curve, but it is intended to clarify, critique, and suggest points for additional research.

The Experience Curve

The experience curve concept resulted from the efforts of the BCG to identify basic rules of success in the management of business enterprises. The key finding of their research which describes the phenomenon itself is as follows: "Costs appear to go down on value added at about 20 to 30% every time total product experience doubles for the industry as a whole, as well as for individual producers" (BCG 1968, p. 12).

Once again, the costs referred to included the full range of costs (R&D, marketing, overhead, and so forth); product experience represented the total number of units produced since the introduction of the product. Although the BCG focused on costs in the statement of the experience curve concept, most (but not all) of their observed data actually related the decline of unit price to increased experience. As the BCG found that these price declines followed a very consistent pattern and that the pattern appeared to apply to a wide variety of products, they concluded that "costs of successful producers must behave in a similar manner. Costs must decline enough to stay below prices" (1968, Introduction). The decline in costs and increase in profits would attract competition, which results in further pressures to reduce prices.

Despite the consistency of the relationship observed by the BCG, they contended that the cost reductions depend on a competent management that actively pursues policies designed to lower costs as volume increases. Management must use this approach with all cost elements and properly relate these elements to each other if cost performance is to be optimal. The failure of a producer to reduce costs in keeping with the industry experience curve will result in an uncompetitive position, and continued inefficiency eventually will force the producer out of the industry.

Hedley (1976, p. 3) pointed to several factors which contribute to the cost reduction performance implicit in the experience curve effect:

1. Productivity improvement due to technological change and/or "learning" effects leading to adoption of new production methods;
2. Economies of scale and of specialization;
3. Displacement of less efficient factors of production, especially investment for cost reduction and capital-for-labor substitution.
4. Modifications and redesign of product for lower costs.

Along with these internal factors, the growth rate of a product is often critical in determining the movement of costs on the curve. High-growth businesses usually find it easier to reduce costs because they have greater opportunities to initiate cost-saving programs and the accumulated experience of the business is rapidly expanding. Real cost reductions are possible for low-growth businesses as well, but at a lower rate because of slower accumulation of experience.

The BCG also argued that "prices follow the same pattern as costs if the relationship between competitors is stable" (1968, p. 19). Data on price and industry experience demonstrated, in general, that prices tend to decline by some characteristic amount each time accumulated experience is doubled. If prices do not follow the same pattern as costs (for example, prices do not decline as fast as costs), the relationship between competitors becomes increasingly unstable, typically resulting in an industry shake-out of marginal producers. Prices decline and eventually stabilize so that they again follow the characteristic pattern of cost decline.

The final major factor which the BCG included in the experience curve phenomenon was market-share. The essential notion is that "if cost is a function of accumulated experience, then profit margin is a function of sustained market share" (1968, p. 23). Businesses with an increasing market-share and, therefore, more accumulated experience can lower their costs faster than businesses which lose market-share. This relative cost advantage results in a greater contribution to profits. At the same time, the interaction of competitors guarantees that superior cost reduction will result ultimately in the elimination of less effective competitors, assuming there is no artificial barrier to competition.

The Experience Curve: Implications

Given that the relationship between accumulated product experience, costs, prices, and market-share exists as proposed by the BCG, there are a number of implications for both business and public policy. In the area of business policy, an understanding of the experience curve phenomenon is particularly useful for the prediction and the analysis of strategic alternatives. Some of the implications discussed by the BCG include:

1. Producers with the highest market-share and, therefore, largest accumulated experience should have the lowest costs and highest profitability.
2. A very high investment can be justified to increase market-share if the product growth rate is high.
3. Reductions in costs and the stability of prices should be predictable.
4. New products should be priced as low as necessary to dominate their market segment and to prevent competitors from gaining experience and market-share before the new product has achieved major volume.
5. A high-cost producer that desires to avoid liquidation should find a market segment of the product market in which the business can be the dominant producer.
6. It is more practical and less expensive to increase market-share by acquiring substantial portions of a growth market than by reducing a competitor's market-share in absolute terms.
7. It is usually more profitable to lead prices down than to follow.
8. Capital requirements should be planned relative to market size, probable price and cost reductions along the experience curve, and the necessity of maintaining a dominant position.
9. The value of market-share can be calculated with enough accuracy to permit determination of the return on investment as a result of any change of share.

10. Export potentials of a product can be approximated by relating comparative advantage derived from experience levels.
11. The cost trade-offs of low labor costs versus concentrated production can be approximated.

The BCG (1968, pp. 48-51) also cited several major implications of the experience curve relationships for public policy.

1. Antitrust policy makers should recognize that competitive relationships are inherently unstable until a dominant (high market-share) producer emerges, and that the consumer is best served by letting (or even encouraging) the emergence of this dominant producer.
2. The experience curve can be used to determine the cost expectations and prices of a dominant producer when effective competition is no longer sufficient and regulation becomes necessary.
3. Free trade can result in great cost savings to individual firms by allowing them to expand volume and go down the cost/volume curve faster.
4. Economic nationalism is very expensive as it reduces the scale of the most efficient national industries and denies access to the products of those producers who are relatively more efficient than the home industry.

The Experience Curve: Limitations

Despite the benefits which the BCG ascribed to the use of the experience curve for strategic decision making, they recognized that there are limitations and caveats. Several of these include:

1. The cost-volume analysis of experience curves is not appropriate for short range analysis or operating controls.
2. Many of the consequences associated with experience curve relationships are only clearly visible on a trend line basis.
3. Experience curves should not be used as measuring devices because of problems with the definitions of product and cost and the measurement of accumulated experience.
4. Inflation may affect the experience curve relationships and should be corrected for when necessary.
5. A successful market segmentation strategy (resulting in the dominance of particular segments) is a viable alternative to total market domination and can result in profitable operations.

The final caveat concerning a successful market segmentation strategy should be emphasized, since the market-share-increasing recommendations of the BCG have been the center of some controversy. Several authors including Fruhan (1972); Chevalier (1972); Hamermesh, Anderson, and Harris (1978); and Hall (1980) have taken issue with the strategic pursuit of market-share in all situations. They have argued that this strategy has certain drawbacks, and, in fact, it may have severe consequences.

While Fruhan (1972) conceded that most companies have committed themselves to strategies designed to increase market-share, an analysis of disasters in the computer, retail grocery, and air transportation industries made him question this commitment. His findings indicated that a firm should attempt to increase its market-share only if it can meet three criteria. First, the company must have the financial resources necessary to gain and support the level of sales implied by its market-share target. Second, the company must still be in a viable competitive position if its expansion strategy is curtailed prior to reaching market-share goals. And third, regulatory authorities will permit the company to achieve its objective with the strategy it has chosen to follow. Fruhan contended that failure to meet any of these criteria precludes attempts at increasing market-share. Based on the results of this study and the BCG experience curve findings, Hofer (1975) hypothesized that firms should try to gain a high share of the market very early in the product life cycle (during market growth) and avoid such a strategy as the industry matures and markets become saturated.

Chevalier (1972) focused on the effects of market-share in several studies of large U.S. manufacturing firms. His results suggested that in industries with little or no technological transfer and in which the actions of a single firm can affect market-share distribution among competitors, businesses should dominate the market segments in which they operate, divest in market segments when market share is small and there are no growth possibilities, and attempt to dominate a small market rather than be a follower in a large one. These findings are consistent with the BCG market segmentation caveat and Fruhan's study in that share-increasing strategies are evidently not appropriate under all environmental conditions.

Strategic actions taken relative to market-share were also the subject of an article by Hamermesh, Anderson, and Harris (1978). Based on a review of business firms operating in different industries, the authors refuted the idea that low market-share firms face only two strategic options: increase their market share or withdraw. They argued, instead, that a business can earn a respectable return on equity, have a healthy profit margin, and continue to maintain strong sales if it exhibits four characteristics. First, it should compete only in markets where its distinctive competence is highly valued. Second, the business must make efficient use of limited research and development budgets. Third, the firm should be content with a small market-share, emphasizing profits over growth. Fourth, the low share business should have leaders who are willing to question the conventional wisdom concerning high market-share at any cost.

Finally, Hall (1980) has concluded from a study of sixty-four firms in eight industries that high market-share and accumulated experience are not necessary for cost leadership in mature markets. He found that four of the eight low-cost producers in the study achieved their lowest-cost position without high relative market-shares. Although Hall takes strong exception to the "doctrinaire" approach of the proponents of the experience curve, his findings may be consistent with the studies discussed above and the market segmentation caveat. The succesful firms in his sample may be dominant in particular segments, thus, resulting in profitable operations.

A number of studies (Schoeffler, Buzzell, and Heany 1974; Buzzell, Gale, and Sultan 1975) have examined the implications of market-share using the PIMS data base. The research has concluded that market-share is a major determinant of profitability as measured by return on investment. While this conclusion appears to be consistent with the high market-share recommendations based on the experience curve, an additional finding tempers the universality of their conclusion. The PIMS studies also found that obtaining a high market-share entailed reductions in R.O.I. and negative cash flow. Consistent with Fruhan, this implies that a firm needs to have adequate financial resources to gain and support the level of sales required for its market-share target. Otherwise, it may be advisable for the firm to exploit its existing distinctive competences and competitive advantages, concentrate on specific market segments, and dominate these segments.

In conclusion, the share-increasing recommendations resulting from studies of the experience curve and the PIMS data base probably should be qualified in stronger terms than the original BCG report. Before engaging in attempts to increase total market share, firms should investigate carefully the requirements of this approach. If this strategy has questionable financial ramifications or if it must be implemented in mature markets with strong competitors, then it may be preferable to abandon a total market domination strategy and emphasize, instead, appropriate segments of the market. This may allow for increased cost efficiency and profitable operations.

The Experience Curve:
Implementation Problems

Hofer and Schendel (1978) have identified several problems involved with the application of the experience curve concept. First, since different stages in the raw material-to-consumer production chain are often at various stages of product/market evolution, it may be necessary to identify different experience curves for each component. Second, some industries use the same components or production processes for different products. It may be necessary to adjust for the effects of these shared experiences in order to predict cost reductions accurately. Third, certain accounting systems may not be organized to supply the historical cost data required to develop experience curves. This also explains the use of price behavior in experience curve research. Finally, Abernathy and Wayne (1974) argued that an overemphasis on experience curve effects can diminish the innovative capacity of a firm as there are increases in work specialization and investment in specialized equipment. It is important to consider each of these drawbacks in the application of experience curves.

In addition to these difficulties, Frahan suggested that an attempt to take advantage of the experience curve phenomenon may elicit an adverse response from the antitrust authorities because of the relationship between price, volume, and the cost effects of experience.

As the name suggests, the experience curve maps out the relationship between the costs of production and the experience the firm has in the production process. Of course, experience can be achieved in two ways. The firm can produce high volume in a short period of time by putting a large amount of capital equipment on line and hiring a large number of workers. The same volume can be produced with fewer men and machines over a longer period of time. Experience can be gained either way and is a function of volume. But the effect of each strategy on price is not the same.

Producing a high volume in a short period of time also implies the need to sell a large amount in a short period of time. The unattractive alternative is to incur high inventory-holding costs. The same volume produced in a longer period of time does not pose the same problem unless the good is very durable and, hence, is not the subject of repeat purchases.

Selling a volume of output may be facilitated in a number of ways. Chief among these are marketing efforts not related to prices (demand stimulation) and pricing policy (increasing the quantity demanded). Selling a large volume over a short period of time can be accomplished by holding price constant and engaging in a great deal of promotional activity; by engaging in no promotional activity and cutting price severely; or by a combination of the two strategies. The latter is likey to occur in most situations, but the relative weight placed on either will vary with circumstances. For example, we might expect a heavier release upon price if the firm is interested in a large volume over a short period of time rather than the same volume over a longer period of time.

Gaining market-share through promotional activities is time as well as resource consuming. Market penetration does not occur overnight since it is often based upon consumer loyalty and repeat purchases. These, by definition, take time. As a result, a firm interested in gaining experience and, hence, the cost savings associated with experience as reflected in the experience curve, would tend to cut prices below production costs in order to sell the large volume produced over a relatively short period of time.

For example, a new or small firm may realize that only one firm will be able to gain a market-share (volume) which will reflect the economics associated with experience. That is, at the price associated with selling the volume of goods required to reduce costs to their "experience-minimum," there may be demand adequate to support but one firm. This simply states in analytic terms that there are advantages associated with establishing market dominance first. However, accomplishing this goal may produce legal difficulties for the aggressive firm.

We have established that gaining experience and reducing costs may require the production of a large volume over a relatively short period of time. This follows for the advantage of getting a toehold in the market early on. Also, we have shown that conducting such a strategy will be likely to require aggressive pricing rather than sole reliance on promotion. In fact, it stands to reason that the firm attempting this strategy price is product *below short-run unit costs*. The optimal price is below this level because future costs will fill with experiences. The price closer must strike a balance between the losses associated with below-cost pricing and the benefits associated with gaining market-share, volume, experience, and, hence, lower average costs. Regardless of the precise nature of the optimal price, it will be below short-run costs and above long-run (experience) costs. Unfortunately, pricing below cost is frowned upon by the Federal Trade Commission and the Antitrust Division of the Justice Department.

The Robinson-Patman Act of 1936 prohibits price discrimination—pricing the same good differentially in different markets. Of course, different prices are allowed if they simply reflect different costs—such as transportation costs. No one would expect a product to carry the same price in a market 1 mile from a plant as in a market 100 miles from the same plant. Moreover, no one should expect identical unit prices for goods sold in one unit lots and one thousand unit lots. The Robinson-Patman Act strikes at price differentials which are not based upon differences in costs. As a result, it will prohibit below-cost pricing of goods because such a practice breaks the link between cost and price which is required by the law. The concern, of course, is that the below-cost pricing is designed, with evil intent, to drive out competition, create a monopoly, and exploit consumers.

There is no question that predatory pricing (that is, below cost) is a possibility. However, as we have seen, below-cost pricing need not be predatory. The intent to drive existing competition from the market is not the motivation behind pricing below short-run costs in order to gain the cost advantages of experience. Yet there is a possibility that others in the market will complain to the antitrust officials and suggest that this is taking place. They may be less efficient or unmotivated in competing for market-share through the exploitation of the experience curve phenomenon. As a result, they are harmed by the aggressive firm that is trying to do so. Of course, consumers ultimately benefit since the lower costs associated with volume-related experience will be passed on as long as there remains some competition in the market. However, antitrust authorities may not see the issue the same way.

Antitrust action is triggered by observed phenomenon which meets certain legal requirements for prohibited conduct. Pricing below cost is such an observed event. Regardless of the rationale behind the practice in terms of the experience curve, the current logic of the antitrust laws will make the implementation of the experience curve phenomenon difficult. Part of the strategy will necessarily involve articulating the logic of the strategy itself.

Bibliography

Abernathy, W., and Wayne, K. "Limits of the Learning Curve." *Harvard Business Review* 52, no. 5 (September-October 1974):109-119.

Akerlof, George. "The Market for 'Lemons': Quality Uncertainty and the Market Mechanism." *Quarterly Journal of Economics* 84 (August 1970):488-500.

Alberts, W.W., and Archer, S.H. "Some Evidence on the Effect of Company Size on the Cost of Equity Capital." *Journal of Financial and Quantitative Analysis* 8, no. 2 (March 1973):229-242.

Alchian, Armen A. "Corporate Management and Property Rights." In *Economic Policy and the Regulation of Corporate Securities*, edited by H. Manne. Washington, D.C.: American Enterprise Institute, 1969.

_____ . "Costs and Outputs." In *Readings in Microeconomics*, edited by William Breit and Harold Hochman, pp. 159-171. Hinsdale, Ill.: Dryden Press, 1971.

Alexander, S. "The Effect of Size of Manufacturing Corporations on the Distribution of the Rate of Return." *Review of Economics and Statistics* (August 1949):229-235.

Andress, F.J. "The Learning Curve as a Production Tool." *Harvard Business Review* 32, no. 1 (January-February 1954):87-97.

Archer, Stephen H. "Financial Aspects of Small Business." *Journal of Contemporary Business* 5, no. 2 (Spring 1976):47-65.

_____ . "Financial Aspects of Small Business." *Journal of Contemporary Business* 5, no. 3 (Spring 1976b):47.

Archer, Stephen H., and Faeber, L.G. "Firm Size and the Cost of Externally Secured Equity Capital." *Journal of Finance* 21 (March 1966):69-83.

Armstrong, M.S. "The Impact of FASB Statements on the Small Business." *Journal of Accountancy* 144 (August 1977):88-90.

Bain, Joseph S. *Barriers to New Competition*. Cambridge, Mass.: Harvard University Press, 1956.

Baumback, Clifford M., and Lawyer, Kenneth. *How to Organize and Operate a Small Business*. 6th ed. Englewood Cliffs, N.J.: Prentice-Hall, 1979.

Baumol, W.J. "The Transactions Demand for Cash: An Inventory Theoretic Approach." *Quarterly Journal of Economics* 66 (November 1952):545-556.

Baysinger, B.D., and Libecap, G. "FTC Deceptive Practices Case Selection Performance: Economic Analysis and Empirical Findings." Working paper, Department of Management, Texas A&M University, 1980.

Beckenstein, Alan R. "Scale Economies in the Multiplant Firm: Theory and Empirical Evidence." *The Bell Journal of Economics and Management Science* 6, no. 2 (Autumn 1975):644-657.

———. "The Economics of Production and Distributions as They Impact a Small Business." *Journal of Contemporary Business* 5, no. 2 (Spring 1976):25-45.

Becker, Gary. *Human Capital.* New York: Columbia University Press, 1975.

Bennet, J.W., and McNight, R.W. "Approaches of a Japanese Innovator to Cultural and Technical Change." *Annals of the American Academy of Political and Social Science* 305 (1956):101-113.

Benston, George J. "Required Disclosure and the Stock Market: An Evaluation of the Securities Exchange Act of 1934." *American Economic Review* 63, no. 1 (March 1973):132-155.

———. "Required Disclosure and the Stock Market: Rejoinder." *American Economic Review* 65, no. 3 (June 1975):473-477.

———. "An Appraisal of the Costs and Benefits of Gout-Required Disclosure: SEC and FTC Requirements." *Law Contemp. Probl.* 41, no. 3 (Summer 1977):30-62.

Berle, A., and Means, G. *The Modern Corporation and Private Property.* Rev. ed. New York: Harcourt Brace Jovanovich, 1968.

Beyer, Janice M., and Trice, Harrison M. "Reexamination of the Relations between Size and Various Components of Organizational Complexity." *Administrative Science Quarterly* 24 (March 1979):48-64.

Blake, H., and Jones, William. "In Defense of Antitrust." *Columbia Law Review* 65 (1965):377.

Blau, P. "A Formal Theory of Differentiation in Organizations." *American Sociological Review* 35 (1970):201-218.

Blau, P., and Schoenherr, R. *The Structure of Organizations.* New York: Basic Books, 1971.

Bloomenthal, H. *Securities and Federal Corporate Law.* Vol. 3B, chap. 14. New York: Clark Boardman Co., 1978.

Blue Sky Law Reporter. Chicago: Commerce Clearing House.

Bork, Robert H. *The Antitrust Paradox.* New York: Basic Books, 1978.

Boston Consulting Group. *Perspectives on Experience.* Boston: The Boston Consulting Group, 1968.

Bowman, Ward S. "Restraint of Trade by the Supreme Court: The Utah Pie Case." *Yale Law Journal* 77 (1968):70-85.

———. *Patent and Antitrust Law: A Legal and Economic Appraisal.* Chicago: University of Chicago Press, 1973.

Brigham, E.F., and Smith, K.V. "Cost of Capital to the Small Firm." *Engineering Economist* 13 (Fall 1967):1-26.

Brown, J. Michael. "Post-Offering Experience of Companies Going Public." *Journal of Business* 43, no. 1 (January 1970):10.

Brozen, Yale. "Competition, Efficiency, and Antitrust," In *The Competitive Economy: Selected Readings*, edited by Yale Brozen, pp. 6-14. Morristown, N.J.: General Learning Press, 1975.

Brunner, Karl, and Meltzer, Allan H. "Economies of Scale in Cash Balances Reconsidered." *Quarterly Journal of Economics* 81 (August 1967):422-436.

Buzzell, R.; Gale, B.; and Sultan, R. "Market Share—A Key to Profitability." *Harvard Business Review* 53 (January-February 1975):97-106.

Caves, R.E., and Porter, M.E. "From Entry Barriers to Mobility Barriers: Conjectural Decisions and Contrived Deterrence to New Competition." *Quarterly Journal of Economics* 91, no. 2 (May 1977):241-261.

Chamberlin, E.H. *The Theory of Monopolistic Competition*. 6th ed. Cambridge, Mass.: Harvard University Press, 1948.

Chandler, A.D. *Strategy and Structure*, Cambridge, Mass.: MIT Press, 1962.

Channon, D. "The Strategy and Structure of British Enterprise." Doctoral dissertation, Harvard Business School, 1971.

Channon, D. *The Strategy and Structure of British Enterprise*. London: Macmillan & Co., 1973.

Chevalier, Michel. "The Strategy Spectre Behind Your Market Share." *European Business* 34 (1972):63-72.

Child, J. "Predicting and Understanding Organization Structure." *Administrative Science Quarterly* 18 (1973):168-185.

_____ . *Organization: A Guide to Problems and Practice*. New York: Harper and Row, Inc., 1977.

Coase, Ronald S. "The Nature of the Firm." *Economics* 4 (November 1937):386-405.

Collins, Daniel W. "SEC Product-Line Reporting and Market Efficiency." *Journal of Financial Economics* 2 (1975):125-164.

Comaner, W.S., and Wilson, T.A. "Advertising, Market Structure, and Performance." *Review of Economics and Statistics* 53 (November 1967):425-427.

Cooper, A. "Strategic Management: New Ventures and Small Business." In *Strategic Management*, edited by D. Schendel and C. Hofer. Boston: Little, Brown & Co., 1979.

Cournot, A.A. *Researches into the Mathematical Principles of the Theory of Wealth*. New York: Augustus M. Kelly, 1960.

Cyert, R.M.; Feigenbaum, E.A.; and March, J.G. "Models in a Behavioral Theory of the Firm." *Behavioral Science* (1959):81-95.

Dewar, Robert, and Hage, Jerald. "Size, Technology, Complexity, and Structural Differentiation: Toward a Theoretical Synthesis." *Administrative Science Quarterly* 23 (March 1978):111-136.

Ferguson, Charles E. *Microeconomic Theory.* Homewood, Ill.: Richard D. Irwin, 1972.

Filley, A.C. "A Theory of Small Business and Divisional Growth." Ph.D. disseration, The Ohio State University, 1962.

_____ . "Alternative Approaches to Organizational Change." In *Contemporary Management,* edited by J.W. McGuire. Englewood Cliffs, N.J.: Prentice-Hall, 1974.

Filley, A.C., and Aldag, R.J. "An Organization Typology," Unpublished research report, 1975.

_____ . "Characteristics and Measurement of an Organizational Typology." *Academy of Management Journal* 21, no. 4 (1978):578-591.

Filley, A.C.; House, R.J.; and Kerr, S. *Managerial Process and Organizational Behavior.* 2nd ed. Glenview, Ill.: Scott, Foresman, 1976.

Ford, J., and Slocum, J. "Size, Technology, Environment, and the Structure of Organizations." *Academy of Management Review* 2 (October 1977):561-575.

Franko, L. "The Move Toward a Multi-Divisional Structure in European Organizations." *Administrative Science Quarterly* 19 (December 1974):493.

_____ . *The European Multinationals.* Stanford, Conn.: Greylock Publishers, 1976.

Friedman, Milton. *Price Theory.* Chicago: Aldine, 1962.

Friend, Irwin. "Economic Foundations of Stock Market Regulation." *Journal of Contemporary Business* 5, no. 5 (Summer 1976):1-28.

Friend, Irwin, and Blume, Marchall. "The Demand for Risky Assets." *American Economic Review* 65, no. 5 (December 1975):900-922.

Friend, Irwin, and Herman, Edward. "The S.E.C. Through A Glass Darkly." *Journal of Business* 37 (October 1964):382-405.

_____ . "Professor Stigler on Securities Regulation: A Further Comment." *Journal of Business* 38 (January 1965):106-110.

Friend, Irwin, and Westerfield, Randolph. "Required Disclosure and the Stock Market: Comment." *American Economic Review* 65, no. 3 (June 1975):467-472.

Fruhan, W. "Pyrrhic Victories in Fights for Market Share." *Harvard Business Review* 50 (September-October 1972):183-187.

Galbraith, J., and Nathanson, D. *Strategy Implementation: The Role of Structure and Process.* St. Paul, Minn.: West Publishing Co., 1978.

Goodkind, J. "Blue Sky Law: Is There Merit in the Merit Requirements?" *Wisconsin Law Review,* 1976.

Gordon, D., and Hynes, A. "On the Theory of Price Dynamics." In *Micro-economic Foundations of Employment and Inflation Theory*, edited by E. Phelps, pp. 369-393. New York: W.W. Norton and Co., 1970.

Goudzwaard, M.B. "Some Evidence on the Effect of Company Size on the Cost of Equity Capital: Comment." *Journal of Financial and Quantitative Analysis* 8, no. 2 (March 1973):243-245.

Graicunas, V. "Relationship in Organization." In *Papers on the Science of Administration*, edited by L. Gulick and L. Urwick, pp. 183-187. New York: Institute of Public Administration, 1937.

Haire, M. "Biological Models and Empirical Histories of the Growth of Organizations." In *Modern Organization Theory*, edited by M. Haire, pp. 272-306. New York: John Wiley and Son, Inc., 1959.

Haldi, John, and Whitcomb, David. "Economies of Scale in Industrial Plants." *Journal of Political Economy* 75 (August 1967):373-385.

Hall, R. *Organizations: Structure and Process*. Englewood Cliffs, N.J.: Prentice-Hall, Inc., 1972.

Hall, R.; Haas, J.; and Johnson, N. "Organizational Size, Complexity, and Formalization." *American Sociological Review* 32, no. 6 (December 1967):903-912.

Hall, W. "Survival Strategies in a Hostile Environment." *Harvard Business Review* 58, no. 3 (September-October 1980):75-85.

Hamermesh, R.; Anderson, M.; and Harris, J. "Strategies for Low Market Share Businesses." *Harvard Business Review* 56 (May-June 1978):95-102.

Hayek, F.A. "The Use of Knowledge in Society." *American Economic Review* 35 (September 1945):519-530.

Hedley, B. "A Fundamental Approach to Strategy Development." *Long Range Planning* 9 (December 1976):2-11.

Henderson, B. *Henderson on Corporate Strategy*. Cambridge, Mass.: Abt Books, 1979.

Hickson, D.; Pugh, D.; and Pheysey, D. "Operations Technology and Organization Structure: An Empirical Reappraisal." *Administrative Science Quarterly* 14 (1969):378-397.

Hirschleifer, Jack. "The Private and Social Value of Information and the Reward to Inventive Activity." *American Economic Review* 61 (1971):561.

Hirschmann, W.B. "Profit from the Learning Curve." *Harvard Business Review* 42, no. 1 (January-February 1964):125-139.

Hofer, C.W. "Some Preliminary Research Patterns of Strategic Behavior." *Academy of Management Proceedings*, August 1973.

_____ . "Toward a Contingency Theory of Business Strategy." *Academy of Management Journal* 18 (December 1975):784-810.

Hofer, C., and Schendel, D. *Strategy Formulation: Analytical Concepts.* St. Paul, Minn.: West Publishing Co., 1978.

Hoffer, E. *The True Believer.* New York: New American Library of World Literature, 1958.

Horwitz, Bertrand, and Kolodny, Richard. "Line of Business Reporting and Securities Prices: An Analysis of an SEC Disclosure Rule." *Bell Journal of Economics* 8, no. 1 (Spring 1977):234-249.

Ijiri, Y., and Simon, H.A. "A Model of Business Firm Growth." *Econometrica* 35, no. 2 (1967):348-355.

James, B.G. "The Theory of the Corporate Life Cycle." *Long Range Planning,* June 1973.

Jensen, Michael, and Meckling, William. "Theory of the Firm: Managerial Behavior, Agency Costs and Ownership Structure." *Journal of Financial Economics* 3 (1976):305-359.

Johns, B.L. "Barriers to Entry in a Dynamic Setting." *Journal of Industrial Economics* 11, no. 1 (November 1962):48-62.

Johnson, M. Bruce, ed. *The Attack on Corporate America.* New York: McGraw Hill, 1978.

Khandwalla, P. *The Design of Organizations.* New York: Harcourt, Brace, Jovanovich, Inc., 1977.

Kimberly, J. "Organizational Size and the Structuralist Perspective: A Review, Critique, and Proposal." *Administrative Science Quarterly* 21 (December 1976):571-597.

Kitch, Edmund. "The Nature and Function of the Patent System." *Journal of Law and Economics* 20 (1977):265.

Klein, B.; Kranford, R.G.; and Alchian, Armen A. "Vertical Integration, Appropriable Rents, and the Competitive Contracting Process." *Journal of Law and Economics* 21 (October 1978):297-326.

Knight, Frank H. *The Economic Organization.* New York: Harper and Row, 1951.

―――. *Risk, Uncertainty, and Profit.* Chicago: University of Chicago Press, 1971.

Koller, R.H. "The Myth of Predatory Pricing: An Empirical Study." In *The Competitive Economy: Selected Readings,* edited by Yale Brozen, pp. 418-428. Morristown, N.J.: General Learning Press, 1975.

Lester, R.A. *As Unions Mature.* Princeton, N.J.: Princeton University Press, 1958.

Liebeler, W.J. "Antitrust and the New Federal Trade Commission." Working paper no. 79-4, Law and Economics Center, University of Miami School of Law, 1979.

Lippit, G.L., and Schmidt, W.H. "Crises in a Developing Organization." *Harvard Business Review* 45, no. 6 (1967):102-112.

Lucas, Jr., Robert E. "On the Size Distribution of Business Firms." *The Bell Journal of Economics* 9, no. 2 (Autumn 1978):508-523.

Machlup, Fritz, and Penrose, Edith. "The Patent Controversy in the Nineteenth Century." *Journal of Economic History* 10 (1950):1.

Malkiel, Burton G. "The Capital Formation Problem in the United States." *Journal of Finance* 34, no. 2 (May 1979):291.

Manne, A.S., ed. *Investments for Capacity Expansion: Size, Location, and Time Phasing.* Cambridge, Mass.: Harvard University Press, 1967.

Manne, Henry. "Our Two Corporation System: Law and Economics." *Virginia Law Review* 53 (1967):259.

McGee, J.S. "Predatory Price Cutting: The Standard Oil (N.J.) Case." *Journal of Law and Economics* 1 (October 1958):137-169.

———. *In Defense of Industrial Concentration.* New York: Praeger Publishers, Inc., 1971.

Megginson, L.C. *Providing Management Talent for Small Business.* Small Business Management Research Reports. Baton Rouge, La.: College of Business Administration, L.S.U., 1961.

Meyer, Marshall W. "Size and the Structure of Organizations: A Causal Analysis." *American Sociological Review* 37 (August 1972):434-441.

Miller, D., and Friesen, P. "Strategy Making in Context: Ten Empirical Archetypes." *The Journal of Management Studies* (October 1977):253-280.

Mintzberg, H. *The Structuring of Organizations.* Englewood Cliffs, N.J.: Prentice-Hall, Inc., 1979.

Mofsky, James. *Blue Sky Restrictions on New Business Promotions.* New York: Matthew Bender, 1971.

———. "Adverse Consequences of Blue Sky Regulations of Public Offering Expenses." *Wisconsin Law Review* (1972):1010.

———. *Market Constraints on Corporate Behavior.* Miami, Fla.: Law and Economics Center, 1977.

Mofsky, J., and Tollison, R. "Demerit in Merit Regulation." *Marquette Law Review* 60 (1977):367.

Mueller, Dennis C. "A Life Cycle Theory of the Firm." *Journal of Industrial Economics* 20, no. 3 (July 1972):199-219.

Mueller, Dennis C., and Tilton, John E. "Research and Development Costs as a Barrier to Entry." *Canadian Journal of Economics* 2 (November 1969):570-579.

Narver, John C., and Preston, Lee E. "The Political Economy of Small Business in the Postindustrial State." *Journal of Contemporary Business*, (Spring 1976):1-24.

Needham, Douglas. *Economic Analysis and Industrial Structure.* New York: Holt, Rinehart, and Winston, 1969.

_____ . "Entry Barriers and Non-Price Aspects of Firms' Behavior." *Journal of Industrial Economics* 25, no. 1 (September 1976):29-43.

Niskanen, William. *Bureaucracy and Representative Government*. Chicago: Aldine, 1971.

Owen, Nicholas. "Competition and Structural Change in Unconcentrated Industries." *Journal of Industrial Economics* 19, no. 2 (April 1971):133-147.

Ozga, S.A. "Imperfect Markets through Lack of Knowledge." *Quarterly Journal of Economics* 74 (1960):29-52.

Pappas, James L., and Brigham, Eugene F. *Managerial Economics*. Hinsdale, Ill.: The Dryden Press, 1979.

Pashigan, Peter B. "Limit Price and the Market Share of the Leading Firm." *Journal of Industrial Economics* 16, no. 3 (July 1968):165-177.

Penrose, Edith Tilton. *The Theory of the Growth of the Firm*. New York: John Wiley and Sons, Inc., 1959.

Pfeffer, J. *Organizational Design*. Arlington Heights, Ill.: A.H.M. Publishing Corporation, 1978.

Phillips, Susan, and Zecher, Richard. *The Securities and Exchange Commission: An Economic Perspective*. Cambridge, Mass.: MIT Press, 1981.

Plant, Arnold. "The Economic Theory Concerning Patents for Inventions." *Economica* 1 (1934):30.

Pondy, L.R. "Effects of Size, Complexity, and Ownership on Administrative Intensity." *Administrative Science Quarterly* 14, no. 1 (1969):47-61.

Pooley-Dias, G. "Strategy and Structure of French Enterprise." Doctoral dissertation, Harvard Business School, 1972.

Posner, Richard A. *Regulation of Advertising by the FTC*. Washington, D.C.: American Enterprise Institute, 1973.

Pugh, D.; Hickson, D.J.; and Hinnings, C.R. "An Empirical Taxonomy of Structures of Work Organizations." *Administrative Science Quarterly* 14 (1969):115-126.

Pugh, D.; Hickson, D.J.; Hinnings, C.R.; and Turner, C. "Dimensions of Organizational Structure." *Administrative Science Quarterly* 13 (1968):65-105.

Robbins, Sidney, and Werner, Walter. "Professor Stigler Revisited." *Journal of Business* 37 (October 1964):406-413.

Robinson, E.A.G. *The Structure of Competitive Industry*. Rev. ed. Chicago: University of Chicago Press, 1958.

Rostow, W.W. *The Stages of Economic Growth*. Cambridge, Mass.: Harvard University Press, 1960.

Rumelt, R. *Strategy, Structure, and Economic Performance*. Boston: Graduate School of Business Administration, Harvard University, 1974.

Salter, M. "Stages of Corporate Development." *Journal of Business Policy* 1 (1970):40-57.

Samuels, J.M., and Smyth, D.J. "Profits, Variability of Profits and Firm Size." *Economica* 35 (May 1968):127-139.

Sargent, James C. "The Federal Securities Laws and Small Business." *Business Lawyer* 33 (January 1978):901-917.

Saving, T.J. "Estimation of Optimal Size of Plant by the Survivor Technique." *Quarterly Journal of Economics* 75 (November 1961): 569-607.

Schendel, D., and Hofer, C., eds. *Strategic Management*. Boston: Little, Brown & Co., 1979.

Scherer, Frederick M. *Industrial Market Structure and Economic Performance*. Chicago: Rand McNally College Publishing Co., 1970.

Scherer, F.M.; Beckenstein, A.R.; Kaufer, E.; and Murphy, R.D. *The Ecomonics of Multiplant Operation: An International Comparisons Study*. Cambridge: Harvard University Press, 1975.

Schneider, Carl, and Manko, Joseph. "Going Public: Practice, Procedure and Consequence." *Villanova Law Review* 15 (1970):283.

Schoeffler, S. "Cross-Sectional Study of Strategy, Structure, and Performance: Aspects of the PIMS Program." In *Strategy + Structure = Performance*, edited by Hans B. Thorelli. Bloomington, Ind.: Indiana University Press, 1977.

Schoeffler, S.; Buzzell, R.; and Heany, D. "Impact of Strategic Planning on Profit Performance." *Harvard Business Review* 52 (March-April 1974):137-145.

Scott, B. "Stages of Corporate Development." Boston, Mass.: Harvard University, Intercollegiate Case Clearing House Report No. 9-371-294 BP 998, 1971.

Seidel, Arthur. *What the General Practitioner Should Know About Patent Laws and Practice*. New York: Practicing Law Inst., 1975.

Sharpe, W.F. *Portfolio Theory*. New York: McGraw Hill, 1970.

Shepherd, W.G. "What Does the Survivor Technique Show About Economies of Scale." *Southern Economic Journal* 33 (July 1967):113-122.

Sherman, Roger, and Willet, Thomas D. "Potential Entrants Discourage Entry." *Journal of Political Economy* 75, no. 4 (August 1967):400-403.

Simon, H., and Bonini, C. "The Size Distribution of Business Firms." *American Economic Review* 48:1 (1958):607-617.

Smith, Adam. *The Wealth of Nations*. New York: Modern Library, 1937.

Spence, A.M. "Market Signalling." Cambridge, Mass.: Harvard University Press, 1971.

Starbuck, W. "Organizational Growth and Development." In *Handbook of Organizations*, edited by J. March, pp. 451-533. Chicago: Rand McNally, 1965.

_____ , ed. *Organizational Growth and Development*. Baltimore, Md.: Penguin Books, 1971.

Steckler, H.O. "The Variability of Profitability with Size of Firm." *Journal of the American Statistical Association* 59 (December 1964):1113-1193.

Steinmetz, L. "Critical Stages of Small Business Growth." *Business Horizons* 12 (February 1969):29-36.

Stigler, George J. "Public Regulation of the Securities Markets." *Journal of Business* 37 (April 1964):117-142.

_____ . "Comment." *Journal of Business* 37 (October 1964b):414-422.

_____ . *The Theory of Price*. 3rd ed. New York: Macmillan, 1966.

_____ . *The Organization of Industry*. Homewood, Ill.: Richard D. Irwin, 1968.

_____ . "Theory of Economic Regulation." *Bell Journal of Economics and Management Science* 2, no. 1 (Spring 1971):3-21.

Stoll, H.R., and Curley, A.J. "Small Business and the New Issues Market for Equities." *Journal of Financial and Quantitative Analysis* 5, no. 3 (September 1970):309-322.

Stone, Alan. *Economic Regulation and the Public Interest*. Ithaca, N.Y.: Cornell University Press, 1977.

Stopford, J. "Growth and Organizational Change in the Multi-National Field." Doctoral dissertation, Harvard Business School, 1968.

Stopford, J., and Wells, L. *Managing the Multinational Enterprise*. London: Longmans, 1972.

Susbauer, J. "Commentary." In *Strategic Management*, edited by D. Schendel and C. Hofer. Boston: Little, Brown & Co., 1979.

Telser, Lester G. "Abusive Trade Practices: An Economic Analysis." *Law & Contemporary Problems* 30 (Summer 1965):488-506.

_____ . "Advertising and Competition." *Journal of Political Economy* 72, no. 6 (December 1964):537-562.

_____ . "Cutthroat Competition and the Long Purse." *Journal of Law and Economics* 9 (October 1966):259-277.

Thanheiser, H. "Strategy and Structure of German Firms." Doctoral Dissertation, Harvard University, 1972.

Tracy, P. "The Dynamics of Growth in Complex Organizations." Paper presented at the 70th Annual Meeting of the American Sociological Association, San Francisco, 1975.

Tullock, Gordon. *The Politics of Bureaucracy*. Washington: Public Affairs Press, 1965.

Viner, Jacob. "Cost Curves and Supply Curves." *Zeitschrift Fur National Okonomie* 3 (1931):23-46. Reprinted in AEA, *Readings in Price Theory*, pp. 198-232. Homewood, Ill.: Richard D. Irwin, 1952.

Wall Street Journal. "Being Small Can Be a Big Advantage to Business Coping with Bad Times." 13 March 1980, p. 16.

Weber, M. *The Theory of Social and Economic Organization.* Translated and edited by A.M. Henderson and T. Parsons. New York: Oxford University Press, 1947.

Weidenbaum, Murray L. "The Costs of Government Regulation of Business," Study for the Joint Economic Committee, 95th Congress, 2d Session, 10 April 1978.

Wenders, J.T. "Excess Capacity as a Barrier to Entry." *Journal of Industrial Economics* 20, no. 1 (November 1971):14-19.

Whitin, T.M., and Preston, M.H. "Random Variations, Risk, and Returns to Scale." *Quarterly Journal of Economics* 68 (November 1954):603-612.

Wilcox, C., and Shepherd, William. *Public Policies Toward Business.* Homewood, Ill.: Richard D. Irwin, 1975.

Williams, Harold M. Testimony Before Senate Select Committee on Small Business, 95th Congress, 2d session, 21 September 1978, p. 576-652.

Williamson, Oliver E. "Selling Expense as a Barrier to Entry." *Quarterly Journal of Economics* 77, no. 1 (February 1963):112-128.

_____ . "The Verticle Integration of Production: Market Failure Considerations." *American Economic Review* 61 (May 1971):112-123.

_____ . "Predatory Pricing: A Strategic and Welfare Analysis." *Yale Law Journal* 87, no. 2 (December 1977):284-340.

_____ . "Transaction-Cost Economics: The Governance of Contractual Relations." *Journal of Law and Economics* 22 (October 1979):233-262.

Wrigley, L. "Divisional Autonomy and Diversification." Doctoral dissertation, Harvard Business School, 1970.

Yamey, Basil S. "Predatory Price Cutting: Notes and Comments." *Journal of Law and Economics* 15 (October 1972):129-137.

Index

About the Authors

Barry D. Baysinger is assistant professor in the Business and Public Policy Group, Department of Management, Texas A&M University. Previously, he was on the faculty of the Graduate School of Business at Indiana University. He received the B.A. in economics from Long Beach State and the Ph.D. in economics from Virginia Polytechnic Institute and State University. His primary research interests concern the effects of state incorporation and securities codes on managerial and firm performance, corporate governance, shareholder political activity, and the function of public affairs in corporations.

Roger E. Meiners is assistant professor in the Business and Public Policy Group, Department of Management, Texas A&M University. He received the B.A. in economics from Washington State University, the M.A. in economics from the University of Arizona, the Ph.D. in economics from Virginia Polytechnic Institute and State University, and the J.D. from the University of Miami, where he was a John M. Olin Fellow at the Law and Economics Center. His research interests focus on the economic consequences of legal and regulatory constraints on business formation and growth. He is the author of *Victim Compensation* (Lexington Books, 1978).

Carl P. Zeithaml is assistant professor in the Business Policy and Strategy Area, Department of Management, Texas A&M University. He received the A.B. from the University of Notre Dame, the M.B.A. from the University of Florida, and the D.B.A. from the University of Maryland. His primary research interests are in the content and determinants of business strategy and the relationship between the organization and its political environment.

HD
2746
B361
WITHDRAWN
From Library Collection

71119

DATE DUE

DEC 18 1987

WITHDRAWN
From Library Collection

Ireton Library
Marymount College
Arlington, VA 22207